CW00495520

Decluttering Workbook

The Essential Guide to Organize and Declutter Your Home and Life With Exercises and Checklists

Lisa Hedberg

Table of Contents

Your Free Gift v
Quote ix
Introduction xi
How to Use This Book xvii

Part One
Preparing for the Transformation

1. The Power of Your Self-Image and the Importance of Goal Setting 3
2. Getting Your Vision Crystal Clear 13
3. Your Habits Reveal a Lot About You! 21

Part Two
Getting to the Root of Your Clutter Issues

4. Clutter is Essentially Decisions You Are Procrastinating On 33
5. Your Perfectionism is Keeping You from Living a Neat and Tidy Life 42
6. Habits of a Neat and Tidy Person 51

Part Three
Decluttering for Life

7. Start with YOU! 69
8. Kickstart the Decluttering Process 82
9. How to Stay Motivated While Decluttering and Using Decluttering Checklists 93

Part Four
Mastering the Art of Organizing and Living Clutter-Free

10. How to Organize Your Home and Your Life 107
11. Routines and Checklists 131
12. Pro Tips on Living a Clutter-Free Life 141

Conclusion 147

Thank You 149
References 151

Your Free Gift

As a way of saying thanks for your purchase, I'm providing FREE downloads of all the exercises and checklists in this workbook. In addition, I'm offering the eBook, *7 Tips to Declutter Your Life,* for FREE to my readers.

To get instant access, just go to:
http://publishingdove.com/

SCAN ME

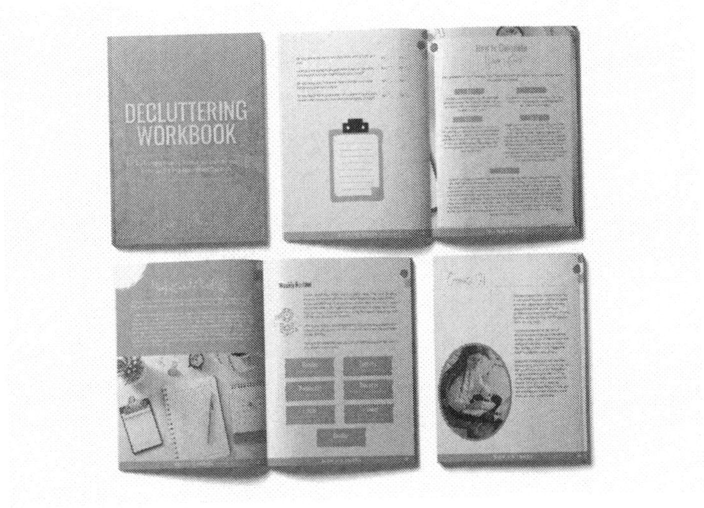

Inside the free download, you will discover:

- A printable format of all the exercises and checklists in this workbook
- A colorful, stunning, and eye-catching exercise and checklist design
- And you will have the option to write in, cut out, and hang or pin the printable worksheets however you like!

Inside the eBook, you will discover:

- Decluttering tools that will save you hours on decluttering your home.
- The secret decluttering techniques that the experts swear by.
- Authentic views, relatable advice, and a fruitful and wholesome decluttering experience from an author who has been in a similar position as you before.
- How to avoid a messy home and even messier thoughts with this book that will guide you through the journey of decluttering your living space and your life.
- And so much more!

If you want to live a happier, healthier life and look forward to coming home every day, make sure to grab your free eBook.

"The journey of a thousand miles begins with one step."

— Lao Tzu

By picking up this book, you have already taken the first step to a new, more organized, and beautiful life. You must feel proud of yourself for this. I certainly am very proud of you!

The life you dream of is possible, and together, we will make it a reality. Come with me, and I'll show you the way….

Introduction

So, let me guess: you've picked this book up because you just can't bear how cluttered your life and your space feels right now. You've already tried getting the clutter bug under control, but it has been impossible to make any lasting changes. You often wonder, *Am I just a messy person?* When you visit someone's beautiful and organized home, you feel a tinge of envy and admiration: *I wish I could be like them and have what they have.*

You may feel like you're stranded inside a dark tunnel with no ray of light visible anywhere, but trust me: you can turn your life completely around. No matter how bad your clutter is, you can clear it. The thought of living in a beautiful, organized home may feel like an impossible dream right now, but it *can* become a reality for you.

How can I say all this with so much confidence and conviction? Because I know what you're going through; I've been there myself, and I am well aware of how excruciatingly painful it is to be surrounded by clutter.

All my life, I struggled with clutter. As a little girl, when I was told to clean my room, I would gather all my scattered toys, shove them in a basket or two, and hide them under my bed. The thing was, I had an idea of what "clean and tidy" should look like on the surface, but I had no clue how to achieve it. My parents told me to clean my room, but there was no instruction on how to go about it. Can you relate to this?

And if you're anything like me, you're also a perfectionist. You want to do everything exceptionally well, or else you just won't do it at all. You've tried to bring your clutter under control, but since you couldn't accomplish all the goals you had set for yourself, you just gave up and resigned yourself to a life of clutter and chaos.

The most valuable piece of wisdom I've learned on my journey of decluttering and getting organized is this: anything worth doing is worth doing poorly. If you haven't cleaned your bathroom because you want to make sure that the toilet is perfectly scrubbed and bleached, the floors are washed, the grout between the tiles is scrubbed—maybe, for once, just start small.

Think of the one thing you can do quickly that will make the biggest difference, perhaps cleaning the toilet. Instead of trying to do the whole bathroom all in one go, just clean the toilet quickly. You can do it in under five minutes. I am not suggesting that you shine it to a sparkle, but a short cleaning session would make a huge difference to how you feel about your clutter problem.

In this book, I will give you clear, step-by-step instructions for getting your space and life organized. If you follow all the steps, you'll get the results you desire! Don't beat yourself up if you don't feel you are doing everything "perfectly." As long as you are taking some action, you are moving in the right direction, and that's worth applauding and appreciating.

I'll give you a mantra that I want you to keep with yourself for the rest of your life. It applies to all areas of life, and it *definitely* applies to decluttering and organizing. *Doing something imperfectly is better than not doing it at all.*

If you can remember this short sentence and truly ponder the great wisdom contained within these few words, you will definitely conquer your clutter and achieve all your other goals in life. A little goes a long way. Even a small amount of progress will compound over time to become a huge transformation.

Take Your First Baby Step Right NOW!

In the first chapter, I'll share with you my formula for setting realistic goals that you can actually achieve. These are the type of goals that make you feel empowered, not the type that leave you feeling inadequate or incompetent.

But first, I want you to complete a task. Why am I asking you to complete a task in the introduction of the book, before we even get to the first chapter?

It's because I want you to start this journey with a win, and this little win will motivate you to take more action because you'll feel a sense of accomplishment right away. You see, in the past, every time you started a decluttering journey, you took your first steps feeling overwhelmed, perhaps even scared. You felt there was a mountain in front of you to climb, and you were quite certain that you'd fail.

This time, I want you to start out differently. I want you to feel like a winner. I want you to be proud of yourself for picking this book and taking the first step.

Perhaps you have been criticized and shamed for being a messy person by people close to you who do not understand what you are going through. You have always wanted to change; you just don't know how. I am proud of you because you are not one of those people who indulge in wishful thinking; by purchasing this book, you've proven that you are among a very small percentage of people who take action to change their life.

To help you feel like a winner, here's what I would like you to do: Think of one thing you have been procrastinating on and do it right now. Make sure it isn't anything too big or excessively time-consuming. Perhaps the task for you would be putting that plate away that's been sitting on your desk for a week, or maybe finally putting your clothes in the washing machine. Maybe that task is cleaning your toilet. Just make sure that whatever the task is, it takes you no longer than 10-15 minutes. If you pick anything more time consuming than that, you will start feeling overwhelmed, and then you might spiral downward into a whirlpool of negativity and self-flagellation.

Once you have completed that task, give yourself a pat on the back and reward yourself in some way. Maybe you can enjoy a cup of coffee afterwards, take the time to simply gaze at the sky, listen to your favorite music, or do something else that feels truly good to your soul.

Feeling good is essential on this journey. If you feel good about yourself and your environment, you will automatically be more motivated to keep it clutter-free. Reward is also a much stronger motivator than punishment. By rewarding yourself for the things you do right, you are building new neurons that will get you in the habit of winning daily. Just remember: life is not about the big wins; it's all about the small wins that, over time, add up to become huge transformations.

Now, go and complete that one task you've been putting off! When you're done, reward yourself, and come back to this book tomorrow. And I really mean it: don't pick it back up before tomorrow. Take one step at a time.

This time, you have me holding your hand, and I promise to take you to your goals.

How to Use This Book

Since this is a workbook, I want you to work with it! If you want, you can read all the chapters at once, then come back to Chapter 1 to start working on the exercises. This would help you get an overview of the type of exercises you'll be performing while working through the workbook's contents. The important thing is to go slow but remain steady with your progress.

I am not expecting you to conquer your clutter overnight or even in a fortnight. You didn't create it in a day, after all. It takes time to create change at a deep, fundamental level.

It may feel tempting to skip some of the exercises, but I would caution you from doing so. Every single exercise has been carefully added to this book. It is there for a purpose. Following the sequence in which the workbook lessons and exercises have been presented will help you get the maximum benefit out of this book.

Also, don't forget that simply reading this book won't help you conquer your clutter problem. Change can happen in your life if you regularly put into practice what you learn from this book. Being neat and tidy is a habit just as much as living with clutter is. You are retraining yourself to act, think, and live differently; it's a process that cannot be hurried. Every single exercise aids this process of transformation.

If you are especially eager to get to the decluttering part, it may feel tempting to skip Part I of the book. But don't do that! Even if you manage to successfully apply the teachings of the rest of the book, your chances of rebounding will be relatively higher if you don't build a strong foundation from which to launch your decluttering journey, which you'll do by completing all the exercises in Part I.

Take your time to absorb the material in each chapter and work through one exercise at a time. Don't be in a hurry to get everything done. At the same time, don't allow yourself to procrastinate. Set a daily target of reading at least a few pages every day and complete the exercise(s) contained within those pages.

Stay consistent and persistent. The neat and tidy life you've always wanted to live is within your reach, and I am here to show you the way!

Part One

Preparing for the Transformation

Chapter 1

The Power of Your Self-Image and the Importance of Goal Setting

"You'll never get organized if you don't have a vision for your life."

— Linda L. Eubanks (Abramson, 2019)

I know what you're thinking: you desperately want to remove all the clutter from your life. Must you read a chapter on goal setting? I understand you, and trust me, I felt the same way. I would pick up a book on decluttering and then immediately start getting rid of things. I just didn't have the patience to do what I thought were superfluous things like goal setting and creating a vision for what a decluttered life actually looks like to me.

So what happened every time? I would go through these marathon decluttering sessions. My space would look neat and tidy for a while, but that never lasted more than three or four days. Clutter would make its way back into my life with a vengeance. The next time I would get around to dealing with my clutter, it always felt more overwhelming than the previous experience. I am not too proud to admit that almost every single time I tried bringing some kind of order to my space was when I expected guests over, or when things had turned so bad, I couldn't live another day the way I had been surviving. Maybe you can relate to that.

Over time, I realized that to facilitate any kind of lasting change, I needed to have a clear vision for what I wanted to achieve and then set goals to turn that vision into a reality. Without a vision and proper goals, we are bound to remain caught up in a vicious cycle of decluttering and slipping back into a cluttered existence all over again. I really felt like a hamster on a wheel trying to break free from my clutter. I was focusing too much on the negative instead of the positive experiences I wanted to create for myself. Yes, all I wanted was to get rid of my clutter, but I never gave much thought to exactly what I wanted my ideal space to look like. Does this sound like you?

Another major impediment for me was my self-image. Our self-image dictates every single experience of our lives. We can't change anything in the external world without first altering the self-image from which every life experience springs forth. Trying to change things in the world without altering the self-image that gave birth to it is akin to fighting your reflection in the mirror. If you want to change what is being reflected back to you, then you must make changes to your appearance. There is no point fighting with the reflection you see in the mirror.

If there is just one thing that you take away from this book, let it be what I will share with you about intentionally designing your self-image. If you can master this idea, then you can change every aspect of your life.

Transforming Your Self-Image

So what exactly is your self-image? Simply put, your self-image is the sum total of your ideas, beliefs, and perceptions about yourself. It's what you choose to believe to be true about who you are.

In most cases, a person's self-image has been formed by the opinion of others. Were you told as a child that you are messy? Did you get yelled at frequently for apparently being terrible at taking care of your things and putting them back in place? Were you labeled as being "untidy," "shabby," "clumsy," or other words that don't do much to lift up any child's self-esteem?

These labels and perceptions seep so deep into our subconscious that we hold on to them as the truth, but none of these labels are true. You don't have to live your life being the person that someone else says you are.

> *"Science and psychology have isolated the one prime cause for success or failure in life. It is the hidden self-image you have of yourself."*
>
> — Bob Proctor ("110 Bob Proctor quotes," n.d.)

Who you want to be is entirely in your own hands, and today, you will make a commitment to become the person you have always wanted to be. The only thing standing between you and the person you desire to be is your attachment to your old self-image. Now is the time to let go of it.

While we're discussing self-image in the context of decluttering and becoming an organized person, it applies to every area of life. I would highly recommend applying the principles you learn in this section to every area of life. I can guarantee you would be amazed by the transformation you'd experience.

By creating a new self-image, you can create a new life for yourself. It doesn't matter where you are in life right now or what your past has been like; the only thing that truly matters is where you want to go and who you want to be. Your destiny is entirely in your own hands!

Exercise 1.1

Date:_________

Write down all the words/phrases you believe to be true about yourself. This can include both positive and negative words (for instance: messy, disorganized, always late, fun, gentle, kind, etc.).

Circle all the negative words/phrases and write them down on a separate sheet. On another sheet, note down all the positive words/phrases you believe to be true for yourself. (The second sheet would be like your cookie jar. Whenever you are feeling low, you can read this and remind yourself of all the wonderful qualities you have.)

Now, for each of the negative words/phrases, create a positive affirmation that counteracts it. For instance, if one of the words on your list is "messy," you can write something like, "I am an extremely neat and organized person." Keep in mind that affirmations are always written in the present tense; it's never "I will be…" It's always going to be "I am…" because you want to start believing that what you want has already happened. It is already your truth. Do this for every single negative word/phrase you have on your list. Make sure that you are using a positive word while writing your affirmation. For instance, don't write "I am not disorganized." Instead, you can write, "I am extremely organized; I have effective systems in place for managing my life and my space."

Once you have written positive affirmations for all the words/phrases, take the papers (except the one where you wrote down the positive words that define you) and burn them. You can also just tear them apart and throw the remains in a body of water. As you do so, say this to yourself: "I am lovingly releasing my old self. From this very moment, I am a different person."

Every day, read the affirmations at least thrice: morning, noon, and night. I strongly recommend you do this practice immediately after waking up and right before going to bed, as those are two times of the day when the doors of the subconscious are wide open. Hence, anything you practice during these two moments will have an amplified effect on your life. You also want to read these affirmations every time your mind starts telling you something negative about yourself. It is definitely going to happen because our self-image has been formed over time through repeated words and experiences. It takes time to bring about a complete transformation.

I strongly recommend you continue this practice for at least 90 days. That may seem like a long time, but I can promise you that your life will not remain the same if you can do this for 90 days.

Exercise 1.2

Date:_________

To begin with, you need to have at least one role model who inspires you and whom you can look up to. Find a person you really admire who has the qualities you wish to have in yourself. This can be someone you know in person or someone you have come across online. It can even be a famous celebrity well-known for their work in the decluttering/organizing space. You can also pick more than one person and note down below all the qualities you admire in them.

Thrice a day, spend at least five minutes every morning, noon, and night learning a little more about them and their habits. Visualize yourself as having the same qualities/habits you admire in them.

This is an extremely powerful exercise. Do it every day for the next 90 days, and your life will change for the better!

Setting Goals that Motivate and Inspire You

> *"All who have accomplished great things have had a great aim have fixed their gaze on a goal which was high, one which sometimes seemed impossible."*
>
> — Orison Swett Marden (Pathak, 2021)

If you're familiar with business and management terminologies, then you likely already know about the SMART model of goal setting. In case you are hearing about it for the first time, fret not. I will guide you through the process of setting SMART goals that you actually end up achieving.

According to the SMART model, every goal must be (Wikipedia, 2022):

Specific: You should know precisely what you want to achieve. So if you want a well-organized, super functional space, then exactly what would it look like?

Measurable: The goal should be set in such a way that you can measure your progress over time. For instance, you can take a "before" picture of your space before you start decluttering. Keep a representative picture handy of what you would like your place to eventually look like. It doesn't have to be exact, but close to your vision of your ideal environment. Every week, you can rate your progress based on how far you have come.

Achievable: If you set a goal that doesn't feel achievable, you'll just end up frustrated, giving up as soon as the first challenge or obstacle arises. Your long-term goals can (and should) be very ambitious, but your immediate/short-term goals should be things you truly believe are achievable for you.

Relevant: Your goal should be relevant to your vision for yourself and the life you want to live. If it's not, you simply won't remain motivated to pursue it with consistency. Your goal should also be something that feels realistic to you. For instance, vowing to declutter your entire house in one weekend is simply unrealistic. More likely than not, you'd end up feeling exhausted and depleted if you tried doing it. Even if somehow you managed to achieve it, you'd end up with a cluttered house again because the clutter problem is as much of a behavioral and attitude problem as it is a physical issue. To shun clutter from your life permanently, you need to work from the inside out. Working on your habits, attitude, mindset, and behavior is the most important thing here.

Also, your house didn't get to its present condition in one or two days. It is simply unrealistic to think that you can get rid of it all in just one or two days. You must stay patient and consistent while building a new self and a new life for yourself.

Time-bound: It is important to set a timeline within which you intend to achieve your goals; otherwise, there simply won't be any sense of urgency to take action. Your goal date should not be something too far into the future. You may modify the date as you get closer to it, but do your best to always achieve your goals within the timeline you have set for yourself.

Exercise 1.3

Date:_________

Write down two decluttering goals: one for this week and one for this month. For instance, your weekly goal might be to declutter one specific corner of your bedroom. Your monthly goal might be to finish decluttering the entire bedroom.

Be sure to write down your goals on paper. Research shows that people have a much higher chance of achieving their goals when they write them down.

Every week, review your progress and set a new goal for the forthcoming week. Once you get into the habit, I want you to also start setting quarterly and yearly goals for yourself. But for now, just focus on setting weekly and monthly goals. If you try doing too many things simultaneously, you'll start feeling overwhelmed, and you simply won't make any progress.

Once you've written your goal down, write down all the steps you would have to take to achieve it. Of course, you can keep modifying the steps as you make progress, but you need some kind of a rough plan to begin with. Without action steps, a goal isn't a goal; it is merely wishful thinking.

Take a piece of thick paper and cut it to the same size as your ATM card. Write your goal on it with a tentative date by which you are planning to achieve it at the top. Keep this card with you at all times; it will keep you focused on what you want to achieve. You can also place the card in a protective plastic cover (like the ones used for keeping name tags safe).

Read your goal every morning, noon, and night to make sure that it seeps deep into your subconscious mind. Every night, write down at least five action steps you will be taking the next day to achieve your goal. The key to having a successful day lies in planning it properly the previous night.

Every day, do the things that you dread the most first. This way, you'll build your confidence by fostering a sense of achievement early on in the day.

Chapter 2

Getting Your Vision Crystal Clear

"Don't let others tell you what you can't do. Don't let the limitations of others limit your vision. If you can remove your self-doubt and believe in yourself, you can achieve what you never thought possible."

— Roy T. Bennett, *The Light in the Heart* (Goodreads, n.d.)

Setting a clear goal for what you want to achieve and the self-image you want to build that complements this goal is the first step toward turning your dream life into a reality. The next step is to turn this goal into a reality in your mind's eye through visualization. The clearer your vision of exactly what you want to achieve and who you want to be, the easier it will be for you to remain focused on your goals. This vision should motivate and excite you so that you take consistent action towards your goals on a daily basis.

Whenever you are feeling unmotivated, you'll bring this vision to the forefront of your mind, and it will provide you with some much-needed motivation to keep moving forward.

Every person's vision for what they want their life to be like, who they want to be, and how they want to live their life will be different. In this section, I'll give you all the important points you need to consider while creating your unique vision.

> *"Vision without action is merely a dream. Action without vision just passes the time. Vision with action can change the world."* –Joel A. Barker (Brainy Quote, n.d.)

Ideal Self-Image Vision

What if you don't know exactly what it is you desire? This is a problem many people have. The interesting thing about decluttering your space is that it affects your mind in ways you wouldn't have deemed possible. Just like how you discover a favorite item that's long been buried under the weight of so much unwanted clutter, you discover that layer after layer of *mental* clutter will start falling away. Once you have gotten rid of all unwanted excesses, you will discover your unique vision for life. It all starts with decluttering your space! The snowball effect happens across all aspects of your life.

But the question is, what should you do for now? Doing the introspective work laid out in the exercises here will definitely help you develop clarity on what you truly want. You can also ask the people closest to you to learn more about yourself. If all else fails, just pick a person you truly admire, observe how they live their lives, and follow suit. Modeling success is often the best way of becoming successful yourself.

As you start intentionally focusing on a vision, you'll develop greater clarity on whether or not that vision truly resonates with you. Also, keep in mind that your vision is not set in stone. You can keep modifying it regularly; your vision may change as you grow. It is important to accommodate those changes whenever necessary.

Exercise 2.1

Date:__________

As I said earlier, your experience of life depends upon the person you are and the person you choose to be. Now, I want you to think about your ideal self—the self you have always wanted to be.

Answer the questions below without restricting yourself in any way. Don't think about how it will never happen or how far away you are from being the person you would like to be. Think of it as a Christmas wish that has already been granted to you. All things are possible, so answer these questions with complete honesty.

1. What does your ideal self look like? What are the predominant thoughts, emotions, ideas, and perceptions of this person?

2. How does this ideal self show up in daily life? What does this person wear? How does this person behave? What kind of body language does this person display?

3. What kind of daily routine does this person have that supports them in being the person they are?

Exercise 2.2

Date:_________

These questions will help you identify what is working for you in your life. Once you know what these things are, you can simply choose to do more of those things and less of the things that don't leave you feeling amazing.

1. If you had a meeting with a very important person, how would you present yourself? (For example, wear your best clothes, do your hair and makeup, etc.)

2. What is different on the days when you are feeling on top of the world? (For instance, do you take out your special China, soak in the bathtub with candles in the background, set the table properly, etc.) I want you to come up with a list of things you do that make you feeling amazing. Don't brush anything off as trivial; what helps you feel good is important. It doesn't matter what anyone else thinks.

3. What are your most prized possessions that you save for special occasions? Make a list of all those things that you believe are meant to be used only on a few occasions.

Ideal Lifestyle Vision

If you want to get rid of your clutter problem once and for all, then you need to know exactly what kind of space you want to be living in. You must also have a clear vision of the kind of lifestyle you want to have.

Exercise 2.3

Date:__________

Think of your ideal living space and your dream lifestyle to answer the following questions:

1. Describe your ideal living space using five adjectives that best define it.

2. What is the décor like? (Is it classic, modern, vintage, minimalist, or something else?)

3. Who is living with you? Or are you living alone?

4. What are the predominant colors that you see around you?

5. What kind of lighting do you have in your living space?

6. How big is your space?

7. How does your space make you feel?

8. How do you begin your day?

9. How do you end your day?

10. What kind of activities and hobbies do you regularly engage in? (For instance, do you spend most of your time in your home office? Do you cook lavish dinners? Do you create artwork?)

11. What does your daily routine look like?

12. What kind of self-care/self-love rituals do you practice every day?

13. What are your favorite items that bring joy to your heart?

Exercise 2.4

Date:_________

Create a vision board by making a collage with images representing your ideal self and desired lifestyle. You can cut out images from magazines, or you can look for images on Pinterest and then print them out. Select only those images that truly speak to your heart and inspire you. If you don't want to print them, then you can just create a digital vision board and use it as your desktop or phone background. Ideally, it should be someplace where you'll be viewing it several times a day. If you decide to print the pictures, make sure that you have them displayed on a poster board. You should hang the board on a wall that you face most often throughout the day, like the wall opposite your work desk.

Chapter 3

Your Habits Reveal a Lot About You!

"Clutter is the physical manifestation of unmade decisions fueled by procrastination."

— Christina Scalise (Abramson, 2019)

I'm sure you know at least one of those people who seem to instinctively and intuitively know how to stay organized. You can grill them as much as you like to find out their secret, but all you'll ever get is, "I don't know. I just do things the way I do." They aren't lying. In most cases, they are really clueless about why they are the way they are—just like you can't quite figure out why you have a clutter problem while others don't. My biggest issue with many of the popular decluttering books on the market is that they seem to have been written by born organized people. They don't empathize much with a person who faces the kind of challenges you and I do. Do you know what I am talking about?

People like you and me feel a strong desire to become organized, but we feel clueless about where to start—and, most importantly, how. For a "born-organized" person, the answers to these questions come naturally. We need a clear sense of direction, guidance, and precise instructions for bringing order to our world.

Fret not; I understand you. I was exactly like you for a very long time. It's only when my life became unbearably dysfunctional because of my clutter problem that I decided I needed to turn over a new leaf. I spent a long time researching and experimenting with different systems. In this book, I will share all my discoveries with you and the system I eventually developed for myself.

Yes, you really need a system for staying clean, tidy, and functional. I wish I could wave a wand and transform your life in an instant. I really do know how much it hurts when you feel burdened with endless piles of clutter. You walk through life feeling jaded and exhausted. Unfortunately, there is no magic wand. You'll have to do the hard work, but with the methods, techniques, and system in this book, you are definitely going to succeed. Just stay consistent and be patient with yourself; even the smallest amount of progress is worth celebrating. Any improvement is better than no improvement.

Born-Organized vs. So-Called "Messy" People

What exactly is the difference between a born-organized person and someone who has been labeled as "messy" and "disorganized?"

> *"Laziness is nothing more than the habit of resting before you get tired."*
>
> — Jules Renard (Brainy Quote, n.d.)

The greatest difference lies in their habits. Organized people have consciously or unconsciously managed to establish successful habits. Becoming successful is not an event; it is a process built on the solid foundation of daily habits.

I've spent a lot of time studying the habits of organized people. I felt a bit embarrassed once I started taking notes and began comparing their habits with my own. But before I tell you more about those habits, let's take a fun quiz to find out where you stand on this habit spectrum right now.

Answer each one of these questions with complete honesty. I know it can feel awkward and embarrassing to admit some of these things, even to ourselves, but if you want to take a quantum leap from where you are to where you'd rather be, you must first have an excellent understanding of exactly where you stand at this moment in time.

The Habit Analysis Quiz

So here we go. Think about each of these questions and circle the right answer in complete honesty. No wishful thinking here; only an honest assessment is allowed.

1. Do you leave your towel on the bed after taking a shower?

   Yes/No

2. Do you wait until the last minute to start packing your bags before a trip?

Yes/No

3. When you return back from a trip, does it take you several days/weeks/months to fully unpack?

Yes/No

4. Are you often late for appointments?

Yes/No

5. Do you refer to yourself as a "messy" person?

Yes/No

6. When you're cooking, do you put everything away before you sit down to eat?

Yes/No

7. Do you hit snooze every morning and go back to sleep?

Yes/No

8. Do you always wake up late and feel like the day has slipped by?

Yes/No

9. Do you often feel overwhelmed by everything you need/want to do?

Yes/No

10. Do you struggle to get back to work after what you intended to be a short break?

Yes/No

11. Are you often struggling to find things at the right time when you need them?

Yes/No

12. Do you have too many single socks in your drawer?

Yes/No

13. Do you have piles and piles of clothes but nothing to wear?

Yes/No

14. Does the idea of doing laundry intimidate you?

Yes/No

15. Does your living space turn into an even greater mess every time you come back with shopping bags from outside?

Yes/No

16. Do you dread stepping inside your bathroom?

Yes/No

17. Do you often turn your underwear inside out and wear them for a few more days because you don't have any clean underwear left?

Yes/No

18. Are you often buying too many of the same things because you can't remember where you kept the original item?

Yes/No

19. Do you often feel like crying because there is so much clutter and chaos around you?

Yes/No

20. Do you feel your life and home has spiraled out of control?

Yes/No

21. Do you feel bogged down every time you step back into your home?

Yes/No

22. Do you leave things lying around after completing an activity?

Yes/No

23. Are you someone who never picks up after themself?

Yes/No

24. Do you leave closets/cupboards/drawers open when you leave the room?

Yes/No

25. Do you feel you look like a mess all the time?

Yes/No

26. Do you feel embarrassed about your appearance when you accidentally bump into someone important?

Yes/No

27. Do you dread having guests over?

Yes/No

28. Would you go on a cleaning overdrive if guests were to come over tomorrow?

Yes/No

29. Do you feel housework is meaningless drudgery?

Yes/No

30. Do you say "yes" to everything when it is practically impossible to complete all the tasks you have loaded onto your plate?

Yes/No

31. Do you struggle with saying "no" to people when they ask you to do something?

Yes/No

32. Do you get up and just start your day with zero planning or forethought?

Yes/No

33. Are you often tripping over your own clutter?

Yes/No

34. Do you feel burdened by the things you own?

Yes/No

35. Do you save your best clothes, China, and other items for special occasions only?

Yes/No

36. Do you remain in your PJs until afternoon or much later in the day?

Yes/No

37. Do you look in the mirror and think about what a mess you are?

Yes/No

38. When you are trying to get your place clean, do you often stuff things in a corner—"out of sight, out of mind?"

Yes/No

39. Do you really *want* to live in a clean and organized home but have no clue how to do it?

Yes/No

40. Do you feel lonely in your battle with clutter and chaos, as if no one understands you and what you are going through?

Yes/No

How to Calculate Your Score

Give yourself one point for every "yes," then tally the final number. Here's what your score says about your habits:

0-5: Well, you are already a very well-organized person. You likely don't need this book, but you can always pick up a few more tips and tricks to level up your game.

5-10: You aren't doing too bad! Forming a few more systems for managing the various aspects of your life will help greatly.

10-20: You feel disturbed by the clutter and chaos surrounding you in some areas of your life. You really want your space to be more functional and efficient but aren't entirely sure how to do it. Well, this book is for you. By doing a little work on yourself, you can become tidier and more productive.

20-30: Alright, you are really struggling with your clutter. Hang in there. I've got your back. This book is for you, my dear! I know it seems impossible to believe that one day you'll be able to live a clutter-free life. May I even suggest that someday, people will be inspired by your example? They'll ask you the same question you have when you come across a super-organized person: "How do you do it?" Trust me; you'll get there. I've got your hand, and I am going to lead you there.

30-40: Houston, we have a problem! My heart goes out to you, my dear. Trust me; I was exactly like you. I felt my entire life was spiraling out of control. Every day of my life was an impossible race against time, and every night, I went to bed feeling defeated. I had so much clutter and chaos around me that, at times, I felt I would cry. Well, there were times when I actually did cry. I wanted nothing more than to live in a beautiful, organized home. At times, that dream felt so far out of reach—but, hey! I finally did achieve my dream, and so will you. For now, you just have to trust me and allow me to lead you on to a new life. If I can do it, so can you! Consider this paragraph to be a warm hug from me. I feel your pain, and that's why I'm here to help you. Buckle your seatbelt because you will experience a dramatic transformation, and it will happen sooner rather than later.

Part Two

Getting to the Root of Your Clutter Issues

Chapter 4

Clutter is Essentially Decisions You Are Procrastinating On

"Clutter is the physical manifestation of unmade decisions fueled by procrastination."

— Christina Scalise (Postconsumers, 2020)

Prior to working as a financial journalist, I worked for a finance company. As was frequently the case, I had once again missed an important deadline. I started working late and couldn't finish on time. My boss was annoyed, and after a long lecture on how I needed to improve my non-existent time management, he asked from the other end of the telephone line, "Look around your office right now and tell me: what is it like?" I went white and silent in embarrassment. To provoke an answer, he interrogated further. "Is it messy or organized?" I whispered as if I was scared to hear the answer myself. "Messy." "I knew it!" he said with exasperation. Then he planted a seed in my mind that has continued to grow since that day. He said, "Your environment is your mind. Clear the clutter if you want to do your job properly! Not just the clutter in your office but also in your home and all your personal spaces, but at least start with your desk and your office. You can't think or plan clearly when sitting at a cluttered desk."

Now *that* was a big idea! I hadn't thought of my personal space and the clutter inhabiting it in those terms. This conversation happened a very long time ago when a mentor I deeply admired had taken me under his wing to work for him and learn the nitty-gritty of the business from him. He really cared for me and thought I was exceptionally creative and original. The only issue was that I needed to become organized, proactive, and disciplined. He did his best to guide me as much as possible, and I valued every word that came out of his mouth as rare gems of wisdom.

Today, I am sharing this idea with you. I have definitely come a long way since those enlightening words fell on my ears. However, it didn't happen in a matter of days or even a year or two. To fully incorporate the wisdom of those words took me several years. But that's because I did not have a workbook like this in my hands that could guide me to take all the steps I needed to take. I knew I needed to get my act together, but the "how" part left me baffled and clueless.

The thing was, my boss was one of those born-organized people. He knew how to keep his mind and environment clutter-free. He could tell me what I needed to do, but he did not understand the struggles of a person who doesn't know how to organize and stay tidy. If you follow all the instructions in this book, then I can promise you that you can accomplish within a few months what took me years.

To begin with, just remember this mantra: *your environment is your mind.* You can't think clearly and calmly in a cluttered environment. Observe your environment, and you will definitely see how the state of your physical space corresponds with your mental state.

Defining Clutter

The word "clutter" is derived from the Middle English word "clotteren," which means "to clot" or coagulate. In other words, clutter happens when there is a blockage or stagnation. No wonder being surrounded by clutter feels like a heavy weight on the soul! Every time we manage to get rid of things we no longer love or that no longer serve us, we feel like a heavy weight has been lifted off our shoulders. We suddenly feel lighter and happier. I'm sure you can relate to that.

In the ancient Chinese art of *feng shui*, this is exactly how clutter is defined. Clutter accumulates as a symptom of what is going inside you. When you feel stuck, indecisive, depressed, or just plain negative, you are prone to accumulate clutter. The catch is that clutter attracts clutter because stagnant energy produces even more stagnant energy. It becomes increasingly hard to feel positive, happy, motivated, and productive in a cluttered environment because the stagnant energy accumulated around you in the form of clutter affects your mental state.

Now, you may be inclined to dismiss *feng shui*, but just think about your relationship with clutter, and you'll realize there is a lot of truth in this ancient Chinese art of harmonious living.

Different Types of Clutter

By now, you have a fairly decent idea of what clutter really is. Let's define it further so you can have set criteria for screening all your belongings to check for clutter. Clutter can be classified as:

Those things that you no longer love or value. Have you ever walked into a beautiful home or maybe even a shop where every object was carefully kept in a specific place? How did you feel being in that space? I am sure you felt uplifted, delighted, and energized.

Now, think about the most cluttered, shabby, and untidy room you have ever been inside. How did that feel? You felt drained, tired, and negative, right? If you take away just one thing from this book, let it be this: surround yourself *only* with the things you love, value, and cherish. Anything else is too large a burden to bear because it is clutter!

Things left in an unfinished state. Anything left unfinished in your environment represents an issue that you haven't dealt with in your life. This could be anything from the painting sitting on your easel for over a month without any set date for getting back to it to the leaky faucet in your bathroom.

Every time you successfully attend to these physical manifestations of unfinished businesses, you'll feel lighter and relieved. I'm sure you know what I am talking about!

Anything kept in a shabby, disorganized, or untidy state. This ties in with the first point we discussed, that clutter is anything that is not loved or valued. Now, it is possible that you *do* love and value your things but aren't showing them the respect that they deserve. You allow them to remain in a shabby, disorganized, and untidy state even though they mean quite a lot to you. In that case, they just become clutter. You may feel joy when you are using them, but they feel like a burden at other times. Eventually, this may wear them out much faster than they are supposed to be used, or perhaps you'll acquire more of the same things because you're never able to find them when needed.

This is why decluttering and organizing go hand-in-hand. You must start out by decluttering. Thereafter, you must stick to a plan for organizing and staying organized. Don't worry; we'll address both of these aspects through this workbook. For now, I just want you to understand that keeping even your favorite things in a shabby, disorganized, and untidy state can make them feel like clutter. This doesn't mean you have to get rid of your favorite things. Definitely not! You just have to organize them and learn to take good care of them. This way, they will serve you and bring joy to your heart for a long time.

Too many objects crammed into a small space. Sometimes a place isn't necessarily disorganized but feels cluttered simply because there are too many objects in too small a space. This can happen when your life or family has grown, but the size of your home has remained the same. The best solution would be to either move to a larger space or rent a storage space where you can store some of your less frequently used items. If you don't have that option, then you can either pare down your belongings or work on smart storage solutions that maximize space. Thinking creatively becomes absolutely essential here.

Smart storage solutions are great for maximizing space, but even this works only to some extent. There comes a point where you feel like you just can't breathe smoothly and freely in a space like that.

Exercise 4.1

Date:_________

I highly recommend you write down the answers to the following questions in the space provided here. Yes, you can mentally answer the questions, but writing has a powerful impact on developing clarity of mind and purpose.

Look around your space and ask yourself the following questions:

1. What are the objects you love/value/cherish the most?

2. Are you taking good care of these objects and showing them the love they deserve?

3. Is your place clean, or is there dust accumulating everywhere?

4. Is your space large enough to accommodate all your belongings?

5. If you neatly organized your space, would it be able to comfortably contain all your belongings?

6. What are the things you no longer use or need?

7. What are the things you should definitely give away to someone else who may find them useful?

For now, I just want you to start building the muscle to start recognizing clutter. Later on, I will give you a battle plan to deal with it all. A problem half-understood is a problem half-solved. So don't take this exercise lightly!

Procrastination Lies at the Root of it All

According to the Merriam-Webster dictionary, procrastination means "to put off intentionally and habitually." Simply put, it is a decision not to deal with things in a timely manner.

How often have you thought you'd start working on the report tomorrow, fold the laundry later in the evening, or put away the grocery bags "at some point?" The more tasks you keep piling up on top of the ones you already have lying around, the greater your clutter problem.

Making decisions in a timely manner requires us to deal with the emotions that arise at the idea of doing something we perceive as unpleasant or cumbersome. It's not that the task is unpleasant or cumbersome—but somewhere along our experiences in life, we came to *associate* it with drudgery.

I have tried many methods of dealing with procrastination. For me, Mel Robbins' five-second rule works the best. In her own words, "The five-second rule is simple. If you have an instinct to act on a goal, you must physically move within five seconds or your brain will kill it. The moment you feel an instinct or a desire to act on a goal or a commitment, use the rule. When you feel yourself hesitate before doing something that you know you should do, count 5-4-3-2-1-GO and move towards action."

Every time I am procrastinating on something, I just do a countdown from five to one, get up, and do what needs to be done. Honestly, it isn't always easy—following the five-second rule does require a certain amount of commitment—but if you stick with it, then it works like a charm. So when I think, *I'll fold the laundry later on*, or, *I'll put the food containers away once I've finished eating my dinner*, I do the countdown and just get things done. Of course, there are certain things that can't be attended to immediately, but you need some kind of a system for managing those tasks, as well, so that you aren't constantly procrastinating on them. In Parts III and IV, we'll delve deep into the system and methods you need to maintain a clean, tidy, and organized space.

For now, just make a commitment to start implementing the five-second rule in your life.

Exercise 4.2

Date:__________

1. Set an hour aside and write down all the things you have been procrastinating on.
2. Pick at least three things from this list and get them done today.
3. Keep adding to this list and regularly review it. Every day, pick three things and get them done. If you have several huge tasks that require a few days or weeks to complete, you can have one big task scheduled for several days and add two small tasks that can be completed in a single day.
4. Whenever you are struggling to take action and do what needs to be done, use the five-second rule. Do a countdown, "5-4-3-2-1-GO," and just take action!

Chapter 5

Your Perfectionism is Keeping You from Living a Neat and Tidy Life

"People always try to be perfect. That's why they don't start anything. Perfection is the lowest standard in the world. Because if you're trying to be perfect, you know you can't be. So what you really have is a standard you can never achieve. You want to be outstanding, not perfect."

— Tony Robbins (AZ Quotes, n.d.)

The root causes of procrastination are a deep-seated fear of failure and an obsession with perfection. As the quote above suggests, perfectionism truly is the lowest standard in the world because it prevents you from achieving anything as you continue putting off starting. You can't be successful at something you never started. On the other hand, you're able to give yourself the satisfaction that you haven't really failed since you didn't start in the first place.

Sit back and think about it for a moment. Are you one of those people who claim to be an "all or nothing" personality?

Are you either going to do something outstandingly and exceptionally well or not at all? And those times when you must get started eventually, do you put off doing things until the last moment because you're afraid you'll get a better idea later and you want to give your absolute best to the task at hand? The way this pans out is that you end up doing things at the eleventh hour—perhaps you pull off one or several all-nighters. You feel you are racing against time; it causes you tremendous stress and maybe even leaves a few dark circles under your eyes.

The question is, does this kind of mindset really support you in the long run? Can you achieve more by delaying things until the last minute? Maybe such a strategy can work up to a certain extent, but you would never realize your full potential and achieve the level of success you desire with such a chaotic approach.

The Cure for Procrastination: Just Get Started

As a reformed procrastinator, I can share with you a mantra that has helped me beat all procrastination. It's a quote by G. K. Chesterton: "If a thing is worth doing, it is worth doing badly" (Society of Gilbert Keith Chesterton, 2012).

I am not suggesting you shouldn't strive to give your absolute best to the task at hand. Far from that, I am suggesting that there is never going to be a perfect time to get started. The potential each human being has for growth and self-improvement is infinite. You will never "arrive" in the truest sense of the word because no matter how far you go, there will always be a new level for you to achieve and conquer. It may sound terribly cliché, but the journey is indeed the reward! But if you never get started, you will never achieve anything. You'll remain stuck in a cycle of failure because you aren't trying to achieve success at all.

I am not suggesting you should not strive for constant improvement, but refinement and modification must happen naturally. At some point, you must just dive in and publish that paper you have long been improving upon or start that exercise regime you have intended to begin but never actually got around to starting. When the desire for improvement becomes an excuse for remaining paralyzed in a state of inactivity, you are only pushing success further away.

The question is, how can you overcome this situation? Again, the five-second rule really helps here. Just think of something you must get done and take the first step. Something very interesting happens once you take the first step: you suddenly develop the motivation to take the second step, the third step, and so on. It is usually the first step that's the hardest. Taking the first step is akin to half the battle won. So just get started!

If you are anything like I was, another issue you have is that you think you'll get started once you have a proper plan. After all, you wouldn't want to take the first step in the wrong direction, right?

I have come to realize this is just another good excuse to keep procrastinating. You don't have to know every single step of the way; you just need a clear picture of the goal you want to achieve and the first step you must take right now. When you take the first step, the second step will become clearer. After the second step, the third step then becomes clearer, and so on. You just have to keep moving forward, and the path will illuminate itself. Just try it. You'll definitely become convinced this is *exactly* how it works.

"The journey of a thousand miles begins with one step."

— Lao Tzu (Brainy Quote, n.d.)

Exercise 5.1

Date:_________

Think of something you have been procrastinating on and write down below how it is making you feel. Record all the negative emotions you're feeling as authentically as possible.

Now, write down the first step you must take to complete this task. You don't have to complete the task; just complete the first step right away.

Once you have completed the first step, write down how you are feeling.

I am sure you'll feel relieved and relaxed as if a weight has been lifted off your shoulders. Next time you find yourself procrastinating on something, go back to your journal and read how you were feeling before completing the first step and how you felt after it. Ask yourself, what is better? How would you really like to feel?

I am sure this will motivate you to take the first step. After taking the first step, it would become easier to continue taking the next step. As long as you are moving forward, you are getting closer to your goals. Don't be too hard on yourself; it's okay to go slow. The only thing you can't do is give up!

I would caution you from reading any further without completing this exercise. Don't allow yourself to procrastinate on it; otherwise, you won't get any real benefits from this chapter. Transformation happens only when you are consistently taking action. Without applied action, knowledge doesn't have much power. Your mind may tell you, *I'll do it after reading the entire chapter, I'll do it tomorrow,* or *I'll do it later,* but don't listen! You are just adding more items to your list of things you are procrastinating on.

Just complete this exercise and then come back to the next section. Go on; do it *right now*!

How to Take Consistent Action and Stay Productive

Nothing frustrates me more than when I am told to do something without any proper instructions on how to actually do it. I'm sure you can relate to that! I know I told you to go and complete the first step for something you are procrastinating on. I also told you that you must consistently take action to keep moving toward your goals. Easier said than done, huh? You are afraid that despite your best intentions, you'll get sidetracked and start procrastinating again. Perhaps you'll convince yourself you are taking a ten-minute break, then procrastinate on getting back to work. To help you remain productive, I am going to introduce you to one of my favorite methods of time management: the Pomodoro Technique!

Now, what on earth is this pomodoro technique?

The technique was developed by a man called Francesco Cirillo. It involves working with intense focus and zero distractions for a period of 25 minutes. At the end of 25 minutes, you get to enjoy a short five-minute break. When the break is over, you get back to work for another 25 minutes. Each 25-minute period of productive work is known as a "pomodoro," which is actually the Italian word for tomato. Cirillo named his time management method the pomodoro technique because the original kitchen timer he was using as a university student to time his work looked like a tomato (Cirillo, 2018).

After completing four pomodoros, you can enjoy a long 20-minute break. After the break, simply repeat the process all over again. You'll be amazed by how much you achieve by practicing this method. Indeed, I find this the best method for staying highly productive throughout the day. Anyone can do anything for 25 minutes; it doesn't sound too hard or eliminating. It is also easier to convince the mind to remain focused for a short duration of 25 minutes than practicing the same for several hours in one go. The mind loves seeing a finishing line; it makes everything seem easier to manage.

You can get your own timer and set it up manually for each pomodoro. Alternatively, you can set up an account on a pomodoro tracker website like the one at pomodoro-tracker.com. By creating an account, you can track your progress throughout the day and review how productive you have been over an extended period of time. At the end of each pomodoro and after each break, you'll be alerted by an alarm.

I recommend that you use this technique not only for your decluttering and cleaning projects but also for other important things. This has been an absolute game-changer for me, and I am sure you'll also see amazing results.

Some rules to keep in mind while using the pomodoro technique:

- Pick one task and focus completely on it.
- Be sure to eliminate all distractions. (No checking messages on your mobile phone or clicking on your inbox, unless it is an essential part of the work you are trying to do.)
- If someone interrupts you for something while you are in the middle of a pomodoro, tell them you'll get back to them in a while. Make a note of their request and address it later on when you have time.
- Pausing or ditching the pomodoro shouldn't be an option you avail of regularly. It should be done only under rare circumstances when it is absolutely necessary to address the unexpected request right away. In that case, I recommend abandoning the pomodoro altogether and starting fresh. The online tool allows you to hit the pause button, but I would recommend not using it. It is better to start a new pomodoro and work for the entire duration of 25 minutes. The only situation in which you can hit the pause button is if you are absolutely sure you won't need any more than 60 seconds to address the unexpected request. Any longer than that, and you'd be better off starting a new pomodoro. Just don't count the abandoned pomodoro when calculating your long break.

- At the end of 25 minutes, take a break, even if you feel like you want to complete the task you are engaged in.
- During the break, don't sit at your desk or do anything mentally demanding like answering important emails. Instead, take a break to recharge and refresh your body/mind. Take a short walk, do some light stretching, drink some water, use the restroom, etc. To stay productive throughout the day, it is very important to move the body at regular intervals.
- Get back to work the moment the alarm goes off. Don't procrastinate or dilly-dally, or the method just won't be effective.
- You can check your email and messages during the long break, but avoid sitting at a desk or remaining glued to the screen. It is better to do something refreshing like a little exercise, having a healthy snack, spending time with your loved ones, etc. Again, make sure that you aren't prolonging the break once the alarm goes off.
- If you finish your task before the 25-minute period is over, you can simply continue the pomodoro by doing another important task. Just make sure that you continue working without a pause.

Exercise 5.2

Date:__________

Start using the pomodoro technique today (or tomorrow, but don't put it off for next week or another time—remember, we are training you to start overcoming the habit of procrastination and perfectionism).

Set the clock for 25 minutes and start decluttering. Don't pause or stop until the alarm goes off. I would recommend doing just one decluttering pomodoro every day as a habit. Any more than that, and you risk feeling overwhelmed. Yes, you can do a decluttering and cleaning/organizing marathon once a week and do as many pomodoros as you like on such days, but as a regular part of your routine, it is better to have only one pomodoro for decluttering/tidying every day.

You can keep another pomodoro for cleaning. Of course, if you have a large house and a fairly big family to look after, you may need more pomodoros for cleaning, decluttering, and tidying. Use your judgment to schedule your pomodoros in a way that best suits your needs and lifestyle. My advice of staying on the conservative side is geared toward a busy executive who already has too much on their plate to take care of. Staying consistent is far more important than having occasional spurts of productivity every couple of days.

Also, start using the pomodoro technique to stay productive throughout the day. It's perfect for managing all types of work, not just cleaning and decluttering tasks. Come on, now; give it a go! You'll definitely feel good about yourself after you realize how much you can achieve in a short duration of 25 minutes.

Chapter 6

Habits of a Neat and Tidy Person

"We are what we repeatedly do. Excellence, then, is not an act, but a habit."

— Will Durant (Brainy Quote, n.d.)

In Chapter 3, we discussed how our habits determine our success or failure in every area of life. Your life is the way it is because of your current habits. You can't change your life without first transforming your habits. That super neat and tidy person you wish you were like has intentionally or unconsciously established a strong set of habits that support them in maintaining the kind of lifestyle they are enjoying right now. You don't have to be born a neat and tidy person to become one. Incorporating the right process, methods, and techniques can enable anyone to get the desired results.

In this chapter, I'll share with you the kind of habits you need to build if you want to become neat, tidy, and organized. I'm not suggesting that you have to do it all in a day; that would only cause pain and frustration. Instead, pick just one or a handful of habits to begin with. Once you have succeeded in consistently practicing the habits you have adopted for at least a week, you can adopt a new one and start working on it. Just remember, practice always makes things better.

Also, as you are building these new habits, be sure to remain patient with yourself. Building new habits requires dismantling the old dysfunctional ones that no longer serve you. This is a process, not an event. It takes time.

According to a study published in the European Journal of Social Psychology, on average, it takes at least 66 days for a behavior to become an automatic part of one's psyche. The study also showed that it takes anywhere from 18 to 254 days for a new habit to be formed (Clear, 2020).

Think of your efforts as wet clay. It takes time to bake them in the sun so that they can become robust pieces of pottery. It would be highly unrealistic to think that if you decided to adopt a new habit, it would start coming naturally to you immediately. In the beginning, you'll have to put in a lot of conscious effort—just like how you were so attentive when you started learning how to drive. Now, you can drive without giving much thought to what you are doing. You know you have successfully formed a new habit once you can practice it without thinking about what you are doing.

Pick Up After Yourself

This is undoubtedly where you need to begin your habit-building journey: start picking up after yourself! If you are dealing with clutter and mess, you are most likely one of those people who leave the towel lying on the floor after stepping out of the shower. You get dressed and walk out of the room, leaving the closet door open. You come back from the grocery store and leave the products lying on the kitchen counter for days, never giving a home to your purchases. Does this sound like you?

From now on, I want you to build new habits. Put things away right after you have completed a task. Don't just shove them out of sight, but let them rest in their proper home. I'm sure you have heard the saying, "A place for everything, and everything in its place."

From the biggest to the smallest object, everything should have a proper place in your home. This way, you aren't scampering all over the place to find things at the last minute. You know exactly where you will find what you are looking for because you have intentionally placed it in its home. Of course, we haven't reached the decluttering and organizing section of this book yet, so it's okay that you aren't abiding by this mantra for now. Right now, I just want to familiarize you with the concept of giving a proper home to every object. Even after you start decluttering, it's not going to happen right away. It will take you time to start living in a home where there's a place for everything, and everything is in its place.

For now, it's enough if you can start picking up after yourself and putting things away after you have used them. If you don't have a proper place for things, you can use a shelf or a basket to put items of a similar type or category together.

Here are some suggestions for how you can start practicing this habit today:

- Hang your towel in a place where it can dry after showering.
- While cooking, put tools and containers back in their place right after using them. Avoid sitting down to eat until you have finished putting everything back in place.
- When you arrive home, be sure to bring only a few bags in at a time. Put all the items away then and there. Bring the other bags in only after you have put away the bags you brought inside. You'll be amazed by how relaxed you feel when you aren't drowning in a sea of shopping bags after coming home.
- Close all drawers, closets, and cupboard doors every time you leave a room.
- Whenever you leave one room, pick up some items that don't belong in that space and place them where they need to go. Get in the habit of constantly assessing what you can take with you in your hands before you're ready to walk out of any room. I find this to be a powerful habit to remain neat and tidy. It only takes a few moments to assess what doesn't belong in a particular space and carry it to another space, and you were going there, anyway.

Exercise 6.1

Date:_________

Look around you. What are the things that shouldn't be around you right now? Select at least five of these items and put them away. Do it right now!

For the rest of the day, do your best to keep picking up after yourself. Continue the practice tomorrow, as well. Before going to bed, set the intention that you are going to stay tidy by picking up after yourself. Setting your intention the night before is a powerful tool for having a productive day. Don't just do it in your head; write it down in a digital or paper journal before falling asleep. This way, it sinks deeper into your subconscious mind, which dictates most of your behavior and thought patterns. If you can stay consistent with it, you'll eventually notice significant changes in yourself and in your life.

For tomorrow, set the intention right now by writing it down here.

Use The 20/20 Rule

The 20/20 Rule is another life-changing concept I learned from The Minimalists' Joshua Fields Millburn and Ryan Nicodemus. According to this rule, whenever you are struggling with decluttering decisions, it is best to let go of the thing you are undecided about if the following two conditions can be met (Fields Millburn & Nicodemus, 2019):

- You can replace the item for less than $20.
- The item can be easily replaced in less than 20 minutes.

Now, I am not suggesting that this can work as a panacea for all your decluttering items—of course not! Some items may cost less than $20 but are special to you for sentimental reasons. Maybe you can replace something in less than 20 minutes, but another copy of the same item just won't feel the same to you. As with anything else, you have to use your judgement here. The 20/20 rule is a great tool to have in your toolbox that may prove useful while making certain decluttering decisions.

Let me give you a few examples of where I applied it in my own life:

- I had 15 coffee mugs sitting on my kitchen shelf when I didn't even drink coffee. None of the mugs were particularly aesthetically pleasing to me, so it just didn't make sense to keep any of them.
- I had more than two dozen cheap $10 t-shirts bought on sale. I didn't like any of them, and they got treated like trash, but I had bought them simply

because they were cheap. We'll talk more about the importance of always surrounding yourself with the things you truly love and value later on in the book. For now, I am just giving you examples of the kind of things you can begin to remove from your life. You are worthy of the clothes that make you feel like a million dollars, not low-quality discounted pieces that you find hard to value and care for.

- The worst places for collecting other people's junk are yard sales—or the modern-day version, Facebook Marketplace. Since everything is so cheap (after all, someone desperately wants to get rid of it), we end up buying things that mean nothing to us. Now, I'm not saying that you can't discover an occasional treasure in someone else's junk, but even the most seasoned yard sale enthusiast would admit that those instances are quite rare. My love for buying cheap items on sale led me to buy too many things that I didn't need at all—case in point, a collection of history books I kept around for two decades, never opening a single one of them. I was keeping them for someday when I may read them. I had to admit that such a day was never going to come, and if it did, I could easily buy those books from a second-hand store at a low price.
- Wasn't I the queen of duplicate kitchen tools? Did I really need 10 potato peelers? What was I planning to do with 20 can openers when I always reached out for just that one?

These are just some examples of things I decided to get rid of. Your list may look similar, or it may be completely different.

Either way, I am confident that you'll benefit from practicing the 20/20 rule to whatever extent you are most comfortable.

Exercise 6.2

Date:_________

You don't have to immediately start getting rid of things. I wasn't ready for it when I first started decluttering. This is where my "command-Z" solution comes to the rescue.

For now, you can place the things you think you should get rid of in a special cardboard box and put it away. Place it somewhere out of sight. If you start missing any of those items, you can easily rescue them. It's like hitting the "ctrl" + "z" buttons on your computer keyboard to undo your last action, hence, the name, command-Z solution.

You can easily undo the act of discarding by rescuing any items you miss since they are still around in a cardboard box. However, most of the time, I don't miss those items. The saying "out of sight, out of mind" tends to be quite true for these types of items. But it is better than taking an extreme step like fully discarding an item when you are not ready to do so. If, after a long time, you haven't missed any of the items that are there in the box, you can go ahead and discard those things.

Get Better at Prioritizing

Most people who struggle with clutter are very bad at prioritizing. Picture this: you decide to finally scrub the walls of your bathroom. You collect all the cleaning supplies and get down to business. Suddenly, the phone rings—it's your mom calling. She asks if you'll join her for coffee this afternoon. You drop everything and start getting ready to go grab coffee with your mom.

I am not suggesting that you form a super rigid schedule with no room for flexibility. That would be just as extreme as not having any schedule at all. What I am suggesting is that you start weighing in on the demands placed upon you on a daily basis and the work you already have on your calendar. Of course, you'll have to start scheduling things in advance on your calendar. We'll discuss more about it in the next section.

Let's look at two scenarios and the different choices you may make:

Say your mom lives close by, and you regularly see her. She casually asks you to grab coffee with her, and you agree even though you have guests coming over in three hours, and your house and bathroom aren't ready to receive them. Since you meet your mom regularly, you have to prioritize here. Preparing your home for the guests coming over is more important than grabbing coffee with your mom on this particular afternoon.

In another scenario, let's say that your mom lives in another city. She is visiting you for a few days and wants to make the most of your time together. Hence, she suggests that you both grab coffee together. In that case, scrubbing the bathroom shouldn't be your priority, as you can do it another day when your mom won't be around.

You have to consider your priorities moment to moment and from situation to situation. The answer is always going to be subjective to you and your goals. The only thing I am suggesting you stop doing is saying "yes" to everything! Your friend calls you up and asks if you'd bake cookies for her son this afternoon, and you say yes. Your father asks if you will pick up his clothes from the dry cleaner this afternoon, and you say yes. Your husband asks if you'll arrange a dinner for his boss and colleagues this evening, and you say yes. Your friend wants to talk to you about her recent breakup with her ex, and you know very well the conversation would go on for at least two hours, and you say yes.

Just look at the number of things you have said yes to! Aren't they going to leave you feeling overwhelmed as if you're racing against time, trying to stretch yourself to impossible limits?

If you want to organize your physical space, then you have to start by organizing your mental space. Everything outside is a reflection of what is inside. To become organized, you have to become really good at assessing what is the most important thing for you to do right now and then focus all your attention on that task. Of course, the answer will be different from moment to moment.

Exercise 6.3

Date:__________

Write down below the most important thing you should be doing right now. Focus all your energy on doing that task. Maybe right now, the most important thing for you is reading this book. In that case, give your full attention to what you are learning here and vow to implement it. It is only through practice that you fully imbibe the knowledge you want to acquire.

Whatever the answer is for you right at this very moment, just make sure that you are devoting 100% of your attention and energy to it right now. Record your answer here.

Plan Things Ahead of Time

I used to be one of those people who woke up without a plan and just attacked the day. No wonder I used to get sidetracked every time an unexpected request came up! I would drop everything to attend to it because I didn't have a proper plan for sticking to whatever task I had at hand.

The best time to start planning your day is the night before. You want to have a vision for how you would like the day to go. It's important to think about the tasks you'll be performing. If you have any appointments, meetings, or any kind of time-bound activity, it must be written down. In the digital age, it's very easy to set a reminder to make sure you get prompted at the right time to show up for your engagements.

Another thing that used to waste a lot of my time was standing in front of the refrigerator, wondering what I wanted to cook. Once I decided what it was I wanted to make, I would try and gather the ingredients, only to realize that I was short on several items. I would run to the grocery store to buy those ingredients only to come back and realize I had forgotten two other things I needed. It took me a long time to understand the importance of writing things down and making proper lists.

These days, I plan the menu for the week every Sunday. I look at all the recipes I plan to make that week and then check my grocery supplies, noting down all the ingredients I need to buy for the week. This makes life a lot easier, and a trip to the grocery store goes by much faster. After all, I am not getting distracted and sidetracked by the plethora of options available at the store. I know exactly what I need, so I stay focused while shopping for groceries. I also vary the menu for the week depending on how busy I will be and how long it would take to prepare each meal. For instance, on those days when I have several work meetings and numerous errands to run, a crockpot meal works better for me. On days when I have a lot of free time to spare, I can afford to prepare a much more indulgent dinner.

You really need to think about your day and assess how busy or free you will be. There are two ways of planning your day: on an hour-to-hour basis or simply having a checklist of things you intend to accomplish on a given day. Personally, I prefer the latter, as trying to schedule every minute of my day really stresses me out. Instead, I keep the list with me, and every hour or couple of hours, I check to see which task I am ready to tick off. Doing the hardest thing on the list first (or at least early on in the morning) really helps in giving me a sense of accomplishment.

Exercise 6.4

Date:__________

Buy yourself a physical planner that looks good and is aesthetically pleasing—or use a digital one with nice features. It's essential that you enjoy the layout and overall look of the planner, as this will increase the chances of you actually using it.

Here are the things you want to plan the night before:

- **Create a To-do List:** Write down all the tasks you want to accomplish. Classify them as P1, P2, P3, and so on based on priorities, with P1 being the highest priority, and P2, P3, etc. as lower priority.

- **Do the Most Important Task First:** Set the intention of completing the highest priority task first thing in the morning. If that's not possible for some reason, then do it as soon as you can. Don't start your day with the easiest tasks; that just increases your chances of procrastinating on the most important task.
- **Decide What You Will Wear:** Think about the activities you'll be performing and decide your outfit accordingly. Check the outfit to make sure that it is clean and wrinkle-free. If not, do whatever needs to be done to prepare it for the next day. Don't put off things like ironing your outfit for the next morning. Life is so much more peaceful when you can take a shower and quickly slip into your outfit for the day. The same goes for the shoes you'll be wearing. I would highly recommend that you wear shoes at home; this really increases productivity. We'll talk more about it in the next chapter. Just make sure that your shoes are also appropriate for the day's activities.
- **Review Your Menu Plan:** I would recommend that you plan your menu on the day you intend to go to the grocery store. This would be every couple of days or maybe even daily for some people. For others, going to the grocery store is a viable option only once a week. Every night, review your menu plan for the next day and think about the time it will take to prepare those meals—or if you'll be buying them, how long it will take to place your order and receive it. You need to have a plan for how you'll fit meals into your schedule. Sometimes, you may have

to switch the meals around if an unexpected demand on your time comes up.

- **Write Down the Timing for All the Important Appointments/Meetings:** You can plan your day on an hour-to-hour basis. I would not recommend it, as I personally find it overwhelming, but if that works better for you, then give it a try. I would recommend simply writing down your list according to priorities and adding only time-bound tasks to your calendar. For instance, if you have a meeting with a client or your son's teacher at 2 PM, write that down. Any task that must be completed at a specific time should definitely be listed on your calendar. I also strongly recommend that you set a reminder using any of the digital apps. This way, you'll be prompted before the meeting/appointment, and missing it just won't be an option for you.

Part Three

Decluttering for Life

Chapter 7

Start with YOU!

"The thing that is really hard, and really amazing, is giving up on being perfect and beginning the work of becoming yourself."

— Anna Quindlen (Mackey, 2022)

So you're ready to conquer all the clutter in your life, but there's so much of it that you don't even know where to begin sorting it all out. Where should you start? My answer is always "start with yourself."

Decluttering or organizing your home isn't the end goal. The *real* end goal is to live in a home that supports you in living a peaceful and beautiful life. What matters most is for you to love yourself and your life. At the deepest, most fundamental level, clutter is a manifestation of your lack of love for yourself. We surround ourselves with an excess of cheap discount-store items we don't really love simply because we don't feel worthy of regularly using the things we truly like. It is difficult to take care of things we don't love or truly appreciate having. And when we fail to care for our surroundings properly, we start berating ourselves. Very soon, the guilt and self-loathing set in, and we remain perpetually trapped inside this vortex of negativity.

The only way to break out of this vicious circle of suffering is by loving yourself first. I know a lot of you are going to squirm at this idea. Isn't it selfish to take time out for yourself when you have a family to tend to? My dear, let me remind you of something: you can't fill anyone's cup from an empty pitcher. To be able to fully support your loved ones, you have to first give yourself all the love and support you need.

Once you start loving yourself by taking better care of your body, mind, and soul, everything else will fall in line. You'll automatically want to live in a clean and organized home. When you feel well put together, you automatically want to put your environment in order.

Loving Yourself is the Master Key to Living a Clutter-Free Life

You must be thinking, *Do we really need to discuss how to love ourselves? Isn't that something all of us know instinctively?* Unfortunately not! Just start paying attention to the constant chatter inside your head, and you'll realize that the way you talk to yourself is so awful, you wouldn't talk like that to even your worst enemy.

The voice inside our head isn't really our own voice. It's a voice we acquired from the authority figures in our early childhood. This voice tells us things like, *You aren't good enough, You always mess things up, You just can't get anything right, You're such a failure,* and the list goes on and on. When you came into this world, you were an innocent little baby. You loved all parts of yourself. I'm sure you have seen how lovingly babies play with their feet and hands. There isn't an ounce of self-loathing or self-criticism in a baby. But as the baby starts growing up, they are constantly bombarded with harsh criticism and verbal attacks.

I am not suggesting that parents, teachers, and other authority figures do this intentionally; of course, they don't. They do it with the desire to help the child and simply because they do not know any other way. This is how the authority figures in their life conditioned them, and they have subconsciously adopted this as the only "right" way to treat a child. But you have this book now, and I am here to teach you a better way. It doesn't matter how much you have grown up; your inner child is still there deep inside your heart, just as hungry for love, support, and compassion as ever before.

The best part is that I'm not just going to tell you to start loving yourself. That sounds all fluffy and nice, but how do you actually put it into execution? In this chapter, I will offer you several practical ways in which you can start practicing self-love and self-care.

And you don't have to start practicing all of it at once. The last thing I want is for you to crash and burn in an attempt to practice self-love. As always, the most important thing is to take baby steps. Adopt just one thing at a time. Once you get comfortable doing one thing, add another, and so on. Don't let your perfectionism (the whole "all or nothing" approach) fool you. One small step at a time is better than trying to jump the entire hallway in one leap. Start small but stay persistent; that's the only way to be successful at anything in life!

Your Self-Love Mantra

In eastern spirituality, a mantra is a phrase repeated often so that it seeps deep into the subconscious mind. Since the subconscious mind dictates our reality, repeating a specific mantra can transform our experience of life. If you have ever been to a yoga class, then you might have wondered why the students and teachers chanted "om" before, after, and perhaps even during the class. The word "om" is a mantra that affects the mind at a very deep subconscious level. Anyone who uses it knows that, at the very least, it relaxes the mind and relieves stress. To make this journey into greater self-love easier for you, I want to initiate you into a self-love mantra. This is how I started my own journey, and I want to pass on this knowledge to you.

I realized that the main reason I had a clutter problem was that I did not love myself enough. Inside my mind was this constant chatter about how I wasn't good enough, I can't do anything right, I am messy, I am disorganized, I can't get my act straight, etc., etc. No matter how hard I tried to change my external actions, nothing would work until I changed my inner dialogue.

In order to counteract the chatter, I created my own mantra. With every inhalation, I would say quietly inside my mind, "I love myself." With every exhalation, I would say, "Deeply, profoundly, dearly." Whenever I started feeling anxious or the negative thoughts became overwhelming, I would focus all my attention on my breath and repeat this mantra.

I want you to start using this mantra from now on. Whenever you find yourself engaging in any kind of negative self-talk, take your focus off the negativity and put all your concentration on your breath. Repeat this mantra quietly inside your mind. Over time, it really starts working its magic. At first, you repeat the words, but you may not believe what you are saying. However, there comes a point through repetition where the words sink very deeply into your subconscious mind. Your subconscious starts believing the words, and eventually, your behavior begins to align with the words you have been repeating.

I'm not suggesting all this can happen in days or even weeks. It takes time for a major shift to occur, but the process of transformation begins the moment you take the first step towards bettering your life. Just try it, and I am sure you'll feel a difference. If nothing else, use it as a tool to distract yourself from negativity, especially in those moments when negative thoughts seem to completely overpower you.

Exercise 7.1

Date:__________

Put this book down for a few minutes and practice the mantra I just taught you. Shift your focus to your breath. With every inhalation, say to yourself quietly inside your mind, "I love myself." With every exhalation, say to yourself, "Deeply, profoundly, dearly." Allow your body and mind to relax fully. Let all thoughts melt away into pure love as you repeat this mantra with each inhalation and exhalation.

Get Dressed Every Morning

This can mean different things to different people. So picture this: how would you dress if you had an appointment or a meeting with someone who is very important to you? You'd put in some effort into looking put together, wouldn't you?

What happens when you make an effort to look presentable and put together? You feel happier and more confident, right?

Don't you deserve to feel this way every single day of your life? Please don't tell me you are so busy that you don't have time to make any effort to look good. As a loving friend, let me say this to you: you deserve better!

You deserve to look good and feel good. We always have time to do the things that are important to us. I am sure if you kept an account of every single hour of your day, you'd find time slots you can spend investing in yourself instead of watching TV, playing games on your phone, or mindlessly browsing the internet. We all do unproductive things, and I'm not asking you to eliminate all such activities from your list. I am simply asking you to prioritize self-care. You are worth the time and energy it takes to look good every day. Your day automatically goes better when you feel good inside, and this is reflected in how presentable you are on the outside.

If being fully dressed for the day implies wearing makeup and jewelry on a daily basis, then start doing it. If, for you, being put together simply means wearing a crisply pressed shirt and skirt, then do that. The whole point is to do whatever makes you feel good, and do it every single day without fail. It baffles me that people put in so much effort to impress the people they do not even like while being their sloppiest and worst around people who are truly important to them, including themselves.

Exercise 7.2

Date:_________

Before going to bed tonight, pick out your outfit for tomorrow based on the activities you'll be performing. Make sure your clothes are clean, tidy, and pressed. Lay them out neatly or keep them on a separate hanger. Getting dressed every morning should be a delightful experience as if you had walked inside a luxury store and found the clothes thoughtfully laid out for you to put on. You deserve this luxury every single day of your life.

Fix your hair and face tomorrow morning. Put in every effort to look and feel your best. You truly deserve it! Do it not because you are going to meet someone special, but because you will be spending the entire day and the rest of your life with the most important person in the world: *you*!

Wear Your Shoes Around the House

So this is a productivity hack I learned a long time ago from *The Sidetracked Home Executive*. The authors recommended getting fully dressed every day, right down to the shoes.

If you're like me, you may just cringe at the idea of wearing shoes that have traveled everywhere outside indoors. To solve this issue, I keep a separate pair of shoes that I only wear indoors. When I'll be spending the entire day indoors, I prefer to wear lace-up shoes. This way, it isn't easy for me to take them off and laze around.

Wearing shoes every morning sends a powerful signal to your brain. The moment you put on the shoes, your mind receives the message that it is time to go to work. You are making a statement to your subconscious mind—it's time for business!

Try this out, and I am sure you'll feel a lot more productive throughout the day. I count this as one of my most life-changing hacks, and I'm certain you'll feel the same way once you've tried it out.

Exercise 7.3

Date:__________

Tonight, set aside a pair of shoes that would go well with tomorrow's outfit. Make sure that the shoes are suitable for all the activities you will be performing the next day. If you'll be spending time both indoors and outdoors, then you may want to have two separate pairs of shoes. You can choose slip-on type shoes you can easily get in and out of if you are concerned about the time it may take to change into another pair of shoes. If you can manage wearing lace-up shoes at least indoors, then I would strongly recommend it. If you don't have a pair, it's a good idea to invest in one. It's not easy being lazy when you're wearing lace-up shoes. Trust me on this one!

Start Using Your Best Things

If you have been drinking tea from a chipped cup, wearing tattered t-shirts to bed, or eating two-week-old leftovers, it's time to remove all these things from your life. Yes, these are the types of items you need to declutter from your life ASAP. You deserve better.

Okay, I get it; your mind is revolting right now. How can you get rid of these things? These are like backups that prevent you from spoiling your precious China or that gorgeous nightgown you bought in France. By eating two-week-old leftovers, aren't you saving yourself time and money?

While using these things may seem practical, they don't leave you feeling good. Hence, they should be eliminated from your life. If you have ever been to a truly luxurious place, didn't you feel like a million dollars because everything around you looked and felt so high-quality?

Why can't you turn your home into such a place? I really feel you deserve it. The only question is, do you feel the same? If not, why? You appreciate such a space when it was created by someone else. Why can't you create such a delightful space for yourself? I'm not suggesting you start buying Mink vases or Van Gogh paintings. The greatest luxury is that of a neat and tidy house, but that goal can only be achieved when you surround yourself with the things you love.

The things you love don't necessarily need to be expensive; they just need to be things you truly value and want to look after. I'm sure you already have quite a few such items. They are most likely stored in the corner of your closet where nobody can touch them, including you. Most people save their best for someday special. They forget that there is only one life we've all got to live. There's no time to put off living for another day. You've got to make the most of every single day!

Think about it: if a very important person were to come over to your home, wouldn't you pull out all of your best things to make them feel comfortable and loved? Aren't you the most important person in your life? Don't *you* deserve to be treated like that special guest?

From now on, I want you to treat yourself like royalty. Start believing that you have been born into a royal family. Every day and every aspect of your life must be completely royal. You deserve to live an elegantly royal life! All the clutter will automatically disappear from your life once you adopt this attitude because clutter is simply an excess accumulation of things that are unloved, unwanted, unappreciated, or not looked after.

Exercise 7.4

Date:__________

Make a list of all your "treasures," including everything that's truly valuable to you, big and small. Pick one item from this list and start using it in daily life. Focus on making every day special instead of waiting for special occasions to celebrate life.

Start Going to Bed on Time

I was really bad at this, and I still struggle with it, if I'm honest. I would often wait until the last minute to complete important tasks. This meant things kept accumulating, and then I would have to do a marathon to complete the task at hand.

I was accustomed to going to bed late at night, and a lot of times, I would pull an all-nighter to complete a pending task with a fast-approaching deadline. This meant I was never well-rested. Every morning, I would hit the snooze button and try going back to sleep. Life felt too overwhelming to deal with. By the time I woke up, it would already be 8 or 9 AM. I felt like I had no control over my life. Worse than that, when I looked in the mirror, I felt awful about the darkness under my eyes. I was barely able to function throughout the day because I was always so exhausted.

The greatest act of self-love and self-care I adopted into my life was to start going to bed on time. Of course, the first night I tried doing it, I just laid wide awake in bed. Instead of going to bed at 1 or 2 AM, I was trying to fall asleep at 10 PM. Obviously, that wasn't going to work. You can't expect the body to adapt to such a radical change on such short notice.

Instead, it's better to gently acclimatize the body over the course of a few days and weeks. So the next day, I tried a different approach: I went to bed half an hour earlier than usual. I did that for a couple of days until I started falling asleep naturally around that time. Once I had established that routine, I reduced the time by another half an hour. I kept repeating the process until I reached my ideal bedtime.

Waking up on time is easier if you go to bed on time. I also prefer to set my alarm on an actual alarm clock instead of on my phone. I find it a much gentler way of waking up; I don't wake up and immediately start staring at a bright screen that pierces my eyes. It also prevents me from checking my phone first thing in the morning, another practice I strongly recommend you give up on. When you start your day by checking your emails and messages, you're allowing the world to dictate how your day is going to go.

Read your plan for the day before starting any activity in the morning. Spend the morning doing things that nurture your soul and give you a sense of groundedness. This should include practicing your self-love mantra, performing your morning cleaning and tidying chores, some form of exercise, and any other activity that recharges your batteries.

You're probably dreading the idea of cleaning and tidying every morning. Don't worry about it; I'll share powerful tools to help change your attitude about cleaning. You'll also learn how to incorporate chores into your routine such that they don't feel like drudgery to you. We'll get to it later on in the book. For now, it's enough if you can start going to bed and waking up early.

How early should you wake up? I really can't dictate that to you. You're the only one who can assess what time is right for you to wake up. You need enough time to start your day on your own terms, to get dressed and put yourself together before you start performing other tasks. The amount of time required for this will be different for everyone, and you need to figure out what works best for you.

Just make sure that you are gentle and patient with yourself. If you're accustomed to going to bed at 2 AM, then setting a goal to wake up at 5 AM starting tomorrow isn't going to be a good idea. Instead, start going to bed half an hour earlier than your usual time and waking up early by half an hour to an hour prior to your usual time. Gradually, keep reducing the time to a point where you reach your ideal sleeping and waking schedule.

Exercise 7.5

Date:_________

Assess how much time you need each morning to perform the activities that nurture your body, mind, and soul. Be sure to account for the amount of time you need to get dressed properly. Set the intention of going to bed half an hour earlier than your usual time, and try to wake up half an hour earlier tomorrow. Place the alarm clock far away from your bed so that you'll have to get out of bed to stop the alarm. If possible, use a physical alarm clock to wake you up in the morning instead of the alarm clock on your phone.

Chapter 8

Kickstart the Decluttering Process

"Don't let the perfect be the enemy of the good. Lower the bar. Actually spending ten minutes clearing off one shelf is better than fantasizing about spending a weekend cleaning out the basement."

— Gretchen Rubin (Hage, 2021)

There are four important terms you need to understand now: decluttering, tidying, organizing, and cleaning. While all four of these terms are closely related, they represent four completely different activities and ideas. Tidying implies "having everything ordered and arranged in the right place" (Cambridge English Dictionary, n.d.). Organizing involves arranging things in a systematic order. Decluttering, on the other hand, involves removing those items from your personal space that no longer serve you or aren't needed anymore. Cleaning is the process of removing unwanted substances such as dirt, infectious agents, and other impurities from an object or environment (Wikipedia, 2022).

In order to live a satisfying life, we have to practice all four regularly. But as a beginner, you don't want to try doing all four together, or you'll burn out and crash. You must begin with decluttering as it is much easier to organize, tidy, and keep clean the things you truly value and cherish than it is to try and practice these methods on items that feel like a burden to you.

Begin with Decluttering

To begin the decluttering process, pick an area of the house that bothers you the most or where you find yourself spending the maximum amount of your time. For me, this area was my bedroom. I decided to start the decluttering process from my bedroom because getting this one room of the house in order would provide me a safe harbor to retreat to every night. Whenever I felt tired of dealing with clutter all day, I could enter my peaceful nest and feel grounded again.

This plan worked out really well for me. So many times during the decluttering and organizing process, I felt overwhelmed. I needed a temporary relief from the chaos that surrounded me. I would make myself a hot cup of chamomile tea and rest on my beautifully made bed, flipping through pages of beautiful homes featured in my favorite home decor magazines.

Ever since I was a little girl, I dreamed of living in one of those beautiful homes where every object radiates with beauty. Somehow, this dream always eluded me. At least by then, I had gotten my bedroom to look aesthetically pleasing, if not exactly like the bedrooms in my favorite magazine. I strongly recommend you pick an area of your home that bothers you the most and that could also serve as a recharging space for your soul.

To start decluttering, first, take every single item out of the space. To make this less daunting, you may want to divide the entire space into several small spaces. For instance, if you are starting in the bedroom, you can tackle the closet in one go. You can also do one shelf at a time, but that may end up taking you too long. You can also perform the decluttering process according to categories.

Under no circumstance should you try decluttering more than one room at a time. For instance, don't try to declutter the kitchen and the living room in one day; that would be too overwhelming. Go slow and steady, tackling just one space at a time.

You are the best person to decide what works best for you. However, if you are unsure, doing your closet first could be a good start. We've become accustomed to acquiring more things than we need or even value in today's times. We buy clothes from discount racks, wear them once, and then those clothes just sit at the back of the closet, completely forgotten.

There is another advantage to tackling the closet first. If you can get your closet to look and feel good, containing only those items you truly enjoy wearing, you'll also feel good about yourself. Wearing clothes, shoes, and accessories that make you look your best provides an instant confidence boost. Dressing up provides the motivation to be more productive. I mean, just try having a super-productive day sitting around in your PJs with unwashed, uncombed hair. You can maybe pull it off for a day or two when you are dealing with a major deadline, but it is hard to stay productive with a sloppy appearance on a daily basis.

Exercise 8.1

Date:_________

Identify the space with which you want to begin the decluttering process. Choose a small area and take everything out of that space. Don't do any more than one room at a time. Make sure that you remove all the items from that space at once for the next exercise.

How to Decide What to Keep and What to Let Go Of

If you're anything like me, it's not enough for you to hear that you must decide what to keep and what to let go of. You need precise instruction on how to arrive at such a decision.

For me, going by my intuition is very important in this process. As I hold each item in my hand, I pay close attention to what I feel. Does it evoke a positive emotional response in me? Am I feeling happy, cheerful, delighted, proud, pleasured? Or does it feel like a burden—something that evokes a negative memory or emotional response in me?

The next thing I ask myself is how I feel about taking care of it. Do I want to take good care of it and treat it with the respect it deserves, or is it going to be tossed around carelessly everywhere? I try to keep only those items I want to take good care of. This is a strong indicator of what I truly value and what isn't so valuable or important to me.

Now, you may be wondering about things like cleaning supplies. You don't feel any particularly positive emotions as you hold them in your hands. For such things, you'll have to consider the value they add to your life. How do they make you feel once you have used them to clean a particular space? If you feel good about any cleaning supply, then it is clearly a keeper. This is how you must assess all your possessions primarily used for utilitarian purposes. Think about the end result you achieve with them, and that should help you decide what to do with them.

Also, with things of a utilitarian nature, proper storage can make them feel like less of an eyesore. When we get to the chapter on organizing, we'll discuss storing your cleaning supplies and other utilitarian items in a more aesthetically pleasing way.

Exercise 8.2

Date:__________

Hold each item in your hands and ask yourself:

- How am I feeling? Am I feeling happy, cheerful, delighted, proud, pleasured? Or does this item feel like a burden, something that evokes a negative memory or emotional response in me?
- Do I want to take good care of it and treat it with the respect it deserves, or is it going to be tossed around carelessly everywhere?
- For things of a purely utilitarian nature, focus on the results they help you achieve and the feelings those results evoke in you. Are those emotions positive or negative?

Decluttering Boxes

For the decluttering process, you'll need four boxes. Mark them as "donate," "alter/fix," "discard," and "ponder." As you go through your clutter, decide whether you want to keep each item. If not, you have to decide which box it should go in.

The donation box will contain all the items that no longer serve you but can prove useful to someone else. The alter/fix box will include all the items that can be fixed or altered—for instance, the shirt you haven't been wearing because of its missing buttons. You feel good wearing that shirt, but the missing buttons prevent you from reaching for it. The discard box will contain all the items that aren't useful to you anymore, and that won't help anyone else, either.

The last box, ponder, is for all those items that you aren't sure about. It is part of the command-Z strategy I shared in Chapter 6. You place all the items you don't use but aren't quite ready to part with in the ponder box. You pack the items carefully to prevent damage and store the box away. If you start missing any of the items in the box, you can go ahead and retrieve them.

Since you keep the box around, undoing the idea of getting rid of that item is easy. If you miss the item, you've established the fact that you truly do need it. But trust me, you won't be needing most of the items you end up storing in this box. I am speaking from experience, and you'll agree with me after finishing all the work we are doing in this workbook.

Exercise 8.3

Date:_________

Get four large boxes and mark them as "donate," "alter/fix," "discard," and "ponder. Go through each item using the questions from the previous exercise and decide which box is appropriate for each item.

You Can Pause, But Don't Stop

When you are looking at heaps and heaps of stuff around, it can be hard to believe there will ever come a point when you've finished sorting through it all. I had similar thoughts when I started my decluttering journey. In fact, this is what every person who has a clutter problem thinks when they first begin their decluttering journey.

You can take a break and sit down to rest for a while, but don't give up. Just keep going through one item at a time. No matter how large your mountains of stuff become, you're still dealing with a finite amount of things. It may take you a long time to go through them, and that is totally fine, but there will definitely come a day when you'll cross the finish line as you decide what to do with your last item of clutter.

There is no specific timeline for how long it should take you to declutter. Every person requires a different amount of time based on the number of possessions they have and how good they are at deciding what to do with their belongings. The good news is that the more frequently you declutter, the better you get at executing the process.

Even though there is no one-size-fits-all timeline for how long it should take a person to declutter, you need to set a deadline for it; otherwise, you'll fall into the nasty tentacles of procrastination and delays. The deadline needs to be realistic. Thinking you can declutter your entire home in a day or two is downright unrealistic, especially if your clutter problem is very serious.

It is better to set aside a certain amount of time every day to devote to decluttering. How long this declutter routine should last depends on how much time you have at hand and the kind of responsibilities you're dealing with. You can try a decluttering marathon for a day or two for a smaller space. Some people have managed to declutter their entire home in a week or two, doing nothing but decluttering all day, every day. This doesn't work for everyone and probably can't even realistically fit into most people's schedules. You need to decide what kind of time you are willing to invest in this and get started. Set a deadline that puts some pressure on you but isn't impossible to achieve.

Exercise 8.4

Date:__________

Schedule decluttering sessions on your calendar and stick to the time you assign to them. Also, set a deadline for finishing the decluttering process for each area and for your entire home.

The Next Step: Organizing

Once you have finished decluttering, it's so much easier (and rather delightful) to organize the things you're left with. We'll discuss various organizing strategies in Part IV of the book. For now, I just want you to start getting in the habit of grouping items of a similar nature together. For instance, all of your tank tops can be held in one place, all your pens and writing tools can be stored in a specific drawer, etc. However, you want to finish the decluttering process first and then move on to organizing what you are left with. Trying to group both of these together is a recipe for disaster. You'll feel confused and overwhelmed as you haven't sorted out quite well what you want to keep with you. It's no wonder the "how" of storing them isn't very clear either.

Once you have things organized, you'll have to maintain a basic tidying schedule to keep them that way.

Maintaining a Basic Cleaning Schedule While You Are Going Through the Decluttering Process

I strongly recommend that you first finish the entire decluttering process and then form a proper routine for cleaning and tidying regularly. Cleaning and tidying take up very little time when we are surrounded only by the objects we love and enjoy having with us.

However, there are two things you must continue doing even when you are going through the decluttering process: laundry and dishes. To keep your house functional even while the decluttering process is going on, you have to regularly do the laundry and dishes. Do not go to bed with dirty dishes in the sink, or they'll never let you have a good night's sleep. Yes, I agree, there are some days when we are all way too tired to do the dishes, and tackling them the next morning makes more sense, but I caution you against making a habit out of this. It never feels good to be greeted by a huge load of dirty dishes in your kitchen first thing in the morning. You deserve to wake up to a clean, fresh kitchen.

Also, as soon as a load of dishes has been washed, try to put them away as quickly as possible. I was personally really bad at this. In fact, I was accustomed to pulling dishes out of the dishwasher immediately before use and putting them back in the dishwasher after use. But this really doesn't feel good. You deserve a beautiful kitchen where all your dishes are stacked properly and aesthetically. It's a delight to use items from such a kitchen!

The same concept applies to clothes. If your home generates a lot of laundry, then you may want to run a fresh load every day. Do it first thing in the morning or as soon as you can get to it. Make sure you aren't getting the clothes out of the washer and dryer only to leave them crumpled. Gather your determination to fold and put them away immediately. This does take discipline, and the five-second rule we discussed earlier in the book is an excellent tool for overcoming procrastination.

The idea behind staying on top of your laundry and dishes is that your house should remain functional even during marathon decluttering sessions. As long as you and your family have clean clothes to wear and food to eat, you are doing well. It's only a matter of time until your home comes into order, and you'll love spending every possible minute in it.

Exercise 8.5

Date:__________

If you have a pile of laundry laying around, take care of it. Wash the dirty dishes that are in your sink. Do these right now!

Chapter 9

How to Stay Motivated While Decluttering and Using Decluttering Checklists

"If you're not using the stuff in your home, get rid of it. You're not going to start using it more by shoving it in a closet somewhere."

— Joshua Becker (Hage, 2021)

Decluttering your home can be an extremely overwhelming project. You may feel like you're trapped inside a never-ending cave with not even a remote glimmer of light in sight. As I said in the previous chapter, as long as you're briefly pausing to rest only to resume the task at hand, you are doing well. No matter how large your mountain of stuff is, one day, you'll get to the very last item.

At the same time, I understand how hard it is to stay motivated while decluttering. There have been so many times when I wanted to throw in the towel and give up the project altogether. Maybe I was just meant to live a messy life, surrounded by mountains of clutter! But I am glad I didn't give up, and you'll be, too, once you reach the end of your decluttering project. No matter how long the journey may take, you're going to get there. You'll see and experience considerable improvement in your clutter situation as you consistently keep moving forward.

Take Before and After Pictures

One of the best ways to keep track of your progress is to take before and after pictures. Before tackling your clutter, take a picture of the space exactly as it is. Many people cringe at the idea of doing this, almost as if they can deny the reality of the situation if they can prevent it from being captured in a photograph.

Something very interesting happens when you take pictures: you can suddenly look at things from a different perspective. It's one thing to be living surrounded by all that clutter and another to look at it like another person does. Pictures are excellent for providing that third-person perspective. Pictures also compel you to observe many details you may otherwise miss while living in that space.

The idea of a space being photographed compels us to adhere to a much higher standard of neatness and tidiness. It is almost like we subconsciously start thinking that we aren't the only ones witnessing our space; through a photograph, anyone can. This makes us a lot more cautious about how we present it.

I recommend you start out by taking a picture of your space exactly as it is, and then as you organize and put things together, take more pictures. This will give you a visual representation of your work, and trust me, you will be enormously proud of yourself eventually.

If ever you feel you have gone back to living in clutterville, you can simply look at these pictures and remind yourself that if you did it once, you can do it again. However, once you have conquered your clutter for good, you will never go back to square one again. Yes, it may seem temporarily that you have gone back to being your old self, living the way you used to, but you will be able to fix the situation quickly. These photographs will serve as strong motivators to remind you of what you have achieved once. If you did it once, you can do it even better the next time.

Exercise 9.1

Date:__________

Take a "before" picture prior to beginning the decluttering process. As you start organizing and putting things together, take more pictures. You can print these pictures or store them in a digital file. Keeping the pictures side-by-side in a collage will help you stay mindful of how far you have come in your journey.

Even after you have completed the decluttering process, I strongly recommend that you regularly take pictures of your space to analyze how you can improve things. Pictures will help you see things you may not otherwise notice while living in that space.

Make it Fun

You are not alone if you're thinking right now that the words "decluttering" and "fun" don't go together. I was the same way. I hated every minute of decluttering! I realized the constant chatter inside my head that kept telling me how I wasn't good enough made things a lot worse for me. I started listening to my favorite music during decluttering sessions to keep my mind engaged in something else. I prefer and would recommend calming instrumental music. This way, you can still ask yourself questions about whether you want to keep or not keep something while allowing yourself to be soothed by the music.

Once you get better at assessing what to do with each item, you can even start doing it on autopilot. Over time, you build the mental muscle memory for it, and you can make the right decisions without having to spend too much time thinking about it. At that point, you can also start listening to things like podcasts, audiobooks, etc. You can very easily double-up your decluttering time as a learning hour.

Exercise 9.2

Date:__________

Play some beautiful instrumental music while decluttering.

A Word of Caution...

One thing I'd caution you not to do is declutter while someone else is around, unless maybe they're helping you out. It is best to declutter alone. If you invite another person to participate in the decluttering process, it may be hard to make the right decisions, as this person may unwittingly influence you. You may hear things like, "You might need it later," "It doesn't look too bad on you," or "I think it looks good on you." It could become difficult for you to figure out how you truly feel about something with this influence. Even worse, once you decide to discard or donate certain items, that person may want to take those items, even if they aren't actually useful to them. If they live in the same household as you, the clutter will continue to remain stuck inside your home, even if it is transferred to their area of the house.

Yes, you can help out a family member if they need your assistance with their own decluttering. In that case, you can teach them to ask the same questions I have taught you to assess what to do with each item. However, I would caution you to keep your decluttering projects confined to your personal territory. Don't try decluttering other family members' items without their permission, no matter how badly their clutter is bothering you. It is possible that what you view as clutter is a collection of priceless possessions for them. You can only inspire others through your example; you can't impose your will or your standards upon anyone.

I know this is tough for a perfectionist like you. You want to declutter every nook and cranny of your house, and it bothers you if even a corner is left as it is. But this is another important instance in which you must give up your perfectionism.

Keeping your relationships harmonious is just as important as living in a neat and tidy home, if not more so. Your family members may or may not be inspired by your example, but you must respect their choices and individuality in every way. You can't force them to adopt a different way of life just because you have. It's better to just be there for them and let them come to you for assistance if and when they want to.

Your example may rub off them and inspire them to also declutter their belongings. For now, you must stick to your area of the house. (If you have small children living with you, that could be an exception. In that case, you can take the liberty to declutter and organize their spaces, too. However, if your children are old enough to have their own likes and dislikes, it would be best to involve them.) As I mentioned in Book 1, it is a wonderful practice to start teaching kids how to stay neat and tidy from a young age. You can also organize fun decluttering and cleaning projects and get the entire family involved (if everyone is on board with it, of course).

If you live alone, obviously, you are free to do whatever you like!

Using Decluttering Checklists

Decluttering checklists always come in handy, but they can be particularly helpful when you feel unmotivated. So if you are not sure which items you should discard, refer to this list to see which ones resonate with you, and get rid of those items. Of course, this could mean discarding the item if it is absolutely not useful anymore or giving it to someone else if they can make better use of it. You can also add them to the command-Z box. However, keep in mind that a lot of these items are better tossed away than stored for later.

In the Closet

- Too many clothes hangers that you never use or need
- Tattered clothes

- Old t-shirts with holes
- Old, worn-out sneakers
- Pieces of jewelry you don't like wearing and that don't have much monetary value
- Socks without their match or with holes
- Anything that no longer fits you and that you don't intend to get altered
- Pantyhose with tears and holes
- Ill-fitting shoes

Linen and Home Decor

- Rugs or any decor item you don't use
- Extra pillows that occupy space in your house but never get used
- Bed linen with holes or significant signs of wear
- Candles that are never lit and also don't serve any aesthetic purpose
- Knick-knacks that are never displayed and usually just gather dust
- Cleaning rags that are too dirty to be washed
- Towels with holes or other significant signs of wear

In the Kitchen

- Any food item that has expired
- Plastic cutlery saved from food deliveries that you won't realistically ever be using
- Plastic containers with missing lids
- Knives that are too blunt to be of any use
- Vacuum flasks that no longer keep beverages hot or cold

- Cookie cutters and other baking tools that never get used
- Bent cake pans and baking trays
- Broken utensils

In the Bathroom

- Expired makeup
- Toiletries that are never used
- Hairstyling tools that don't work anymore
- Stained or worn-out shower curtains
- Expired medicine
- Dried-up nail polish
- Expired sunscreen and other grooming products
- Makeup that has never been used and likely never going to be used
- Empty bottles and containers of used-up products
- Melted soap
- Unused cologne and perfume

In the Bedroom and Living Room

- Items tucked under the bed that are never actually used
- Melted candles that aren't usable anymore
- Broken furniture that can't be fixed
- Dying plants
- Wilted flowers
- Broken decor pieces

Paper Clutter

- Old bills and paychecks that are never going to be needed (especially if you have them in digital format, anyway)
- Old newspaper
- Outdated calendars
- Notebooks you don't use and that just aren't aesthetically pleasing enough
- Expired coupons
- Used-up planners
- Ticket stubs
- Take-out menus (you can find the most up-to-date ones with the click of a button)
- Grocery store newsletters
- Old magazines you haven't flipped through in ages
- Books you are never going to read or read again

Technology and Entertainment

- Mobile phones/laptops that don't work
- Earphones you never use
- Old CDs and VHS tapes, especially if you don't have a player for them
- Toys that no one plays with
- Puzzles or other games with missing pieces
- Cords that aren't compatible with any of your current devices
- Chargers that no longer work
- Old screen protectors and phone covers
- Stuffed animals that neither you nor family members like having around
- Old TVs that don't function or are never used
- Video games and/or board games that no one really plays with

Miscellaneous

- Projects left in an unfinished state
- Old, dried-out paint
- Old product boxes with the contents used up
- Broken flower pots
- Anything that doesn't work anymore (either get it fixed or get rid of it!)
- Expired cleaning supplies
- Keychains you don't use
- Refrigerator magnets that don't make you happy but make your refrigerator look cluttered
- Duplicate tape measures
- Old party supplies
- Tools and machinery that are rusting
- Seasonal holiday decor that is never actually used

What to Do with Sentimental Items

If you've read the first book, you already know what I have to say on this subject. I know parting with sentimental items can be extremely tough. We feel guilty classifying something that has been lovingly given or passed on to us as clutter. However, the truth is that if something is never used or truly valued, it is clutter. This doesn't diminish the value or importance of the person who has given the item to us. We must learn to separate our feelings for the person from our feelings for the item we've received from that person. They are not one and the same thing; the two must never be confused together.

In Book 1, I suggested that you give the item away to someone who would get better use out of it. If the idea of giving the item away still doesn't appeal to you, then I have a few more suggestions for you. There are two things you can do:

- Take a picture, and then give the item away. This way, you'll always have the memory of the item with you, and you can recall all the wonderful emotions you feel towards the person by looking at the picture of their gift to you.
- Try to put the item to alternative uses. For instance, a coffee mug you don't like drinking coffee out of can serve as a stationary holder on your work table. Similarly, a dress you aren't ever going to wear can become a cushion cover (if you know how to sew or can take it to a seamstress). Every item can be put to some kind of alternative use; think creatively and you'll be able to come up with something.

Exercise 9.3

Date:__________

Create a list of all the sentimental items that don't make you happy but are difficult to part with. Once you have the list ready, write down 1-3 alternative uses to which you can put each item.

Part Four

Mastering the Art of Organizing and Living Clutter-Free

Chapter 10

How to Organize Your Home and Your Life

"For every minute spent organizing, an hour is earned."

— Benjamin Franklin (Order Your Life, 2018)

The next most important task after decluttering is organizing. Through organizing, you want to bring a sense of order and functionality to your space. Before you begin organizing your belongings, create a vision for how you would like to approach your space.

Here are some questions to think about before you start organizing:

- How can you make the best use of the space available to you? Are you storing items that fit appropriately in the space available to you, or do you have smaller items taking up lots of space when that space can be used to store bigger items?

- What are the ways in which you can maximize space? For instance, you can use closet dividers, shelf organizers, and hanging organizers to maximize the space in your closet.

Place Your Most Frequently Used Items in an Accessible Location

The most important thing to remember with organizing is that you want to place your most frequently used items in the front, and those items you don't reach out for often at an intuitive location. You want to be able to find the latter when you need it, but you don't need to have it at an easy-to-reach location. For instance, in my closets and cupboards, I place the items I reach out for daily or very frequently at eye level. I reserve the top and bottom shelves for items I don't use as frequently. I still do my best to keep items of a similar type grouped together. This way, I know exactly where I can find an item when I am looking for it.

Important Organizational Methods and Techniques

There are several very simple tricks and methods that you can use to organize your space. I'm going to share some of my most favorite methods here.

Labeling

This is one of the most effective ways of distinguishing items from each other. You can use different types of labels. For instance, I love using chalkboard-type label stickers in my pantry. You can erase and rewrite these types of labels as they come with chalk or a chalk-style pen. But to be very honest, they don't erase that well. It's best to write just once and store your desired item in the container labeled for it. If you must erase the writing, it would be a good idea to use some glass cleaning spray and wipe off the writing with a microfiber cloth.

I also strongly recommend getting a label maker. They aren't that expensive and can be easily bought online. I've had mine for a very long time, and it has turned out to be a worthy investment. As much as I love labeling things, I would caution you against over-labeling, or your home will start resembling a meticulous instruction manual!

It is better to do the labeling in more subtle ways:

- **Labeling in hidden places:** You can place the labels in areas that aren't directly visible to the eye. For instance, inside a cabinet, you can place the labels on the top surface of the shelf. Similarly, you can place the label under the box or in any other area where you will have to make a slight effort to find the label, but it shouldn't be too much of a strain.
- **Buy organizers with built-in slots for labels:** Labels look a lot more natural inside the built-in labeling slots of organizers.
- **Buy pre-labeled organizers:** This is undoubtedly the most elegant option. You can buy containers for specific purposes that have been pre-labeled, for instance, a beautiful jar with "sugar" written on it or a cookie jar that has cookies drawn all over it.

Color Coding

This is another excellent method for organizing different items categorically. You can buy bins in different colors and use each color to store items belonging to a specific category. For instance, I store all my heat-styling tools in a blue bin, but my hair products go inside a purple bin. Having separate colors for these different categories helps me easily find the item I am looking for.

Color coding is also excellent for helping children stay organized. You can assign different colored storage containers to each child. Even very small children will be able to keep their items organized when they know in which color container all their items should go into.

Using Transparent Organizers

Using transparent organizers is excellent for keeping items visible and, hence, easily accessible. You get to "label" the items without using an actual label. This method works really well for organizing spaces where you'd regularly be changing labels. For instance, you can get clear containers for organizing different items in your refrigerator.

Stack Items Vertically Instead of Horizontally

This is something I learned from Marie Kondo. Marie advises you to keep folded items vertically stacked together instead of horizontally on top of one another. This prevents the disaster that happens when items are stacked horizontally on top of one another: you try pulling one item out, and everything else falls out of place, as well. When items are vertically stacked together inside a bin or drawer, there isn't any possibility of the other items falling apart every time you pull one item out.

Marie Kondo recommends a very specific method of folding which you can easily learn from her YouTube videos. It's definitely worth learning her folding techniques for various clothing items.

Use Bins and Baskets Generously

I seriously feel that I can never have too many organizers. No matter how many organizers I buy, I end up using all of them. You could say I'm addicted to organizers! While there are organizers available for every possible purpose from neatly storing your cleaning supplies to organizing your tech gadgets, I suggest you start with the very basics. Your first goal should be to acquire plastic boxes, bins, and baskets in various colors. Just make sure the colors you place together in any space go harmoniously together. You may even want to adopt a monochrome color theme for certain areas, using organizational supplies in just one color.

The easiest way to make any space look put-together is to place items belonging to a specific category inside a bin or basket. This also makes cleaning closets and cupboard surfaces a breeze because you can very easily pull everything out as all things will be stored in their respective baskets. This is one of my favorite hacks for reducing cleaning time.

Exercise 10.1

Date:_________

Now, it's time to determine what kind of organizational supplies you should shop for. If you don't have the budget for it right now, you can use whatever boxes and cartons you have lying around the house. To make such boxes more aesthetically pleasing, you can cover them with colorful craft paper. No matter your budget, there is no excuse for not putting in the effort to get organized. If you don't have ample money to buy new supplies for organizing, you can use your creativity to make your own. There are plenty of tutorials online that can instruct you on how to do it.

If you can spare money on new organizers, there's nothing like it. You can get very cheap plastic organizers at discount stores. Most of them look decent and work perfectly well. Organizers meant for specific purposes can be quite expensive; I suggest you save those for last. Start by purchasing bins, boxes, and baskets. These are going to be the most versatile organizers you'll end up using everywhere in your house.

Organizational Tools and Supplies Checklist

Think about one space at a time and write down the number of each item you'll need. Of course, tools like a label maker need to be bought only once, but the tape needed for it may have to be replenished from time to time. As for supplies like baskets, bins, and boxes, you'll need them according to the space you are trying to organize.

I suggest you make photocopies of the checklist below so that you can use a separate sheet for each space you are working on. (Don't forget to download the free printable exercises and checklists; the link is at the front of this book!) Mark a ✓ next to the item that you intend to buy or that you already own. In the blank space under the item name, you can write down the number of each item you'll need. This way, you'll have all the supplies and tools at hand when working on organizing a particular space.

Tools

- Label stickers

Number: ___

- CD marker pens for writing on label stickers

Number: ___

- Chalkboard stickers

Number: ___

- Chalkboard pencil for writing on blackboard stickers

Number: 1

- Label maker

Number: 1

- Label maker tape

Number: ___

- Scissors

Number: 1 pair

Supplies

Along with the total number of items you need, I would also recommend writing down the color(s) and size(s) in which you intend to get them. If you aren't sure what each of these items is, you can look them up online. As I said earlier, pick only what suits you.

- Baskets

Number: ___ Colors: ____________________

- Bins

Number: ___ Colors: ____________________

- Boxes

Number: ___ Colors: ____________________

- Clear baskets

Number: ___ Colors: ____________________

- Clear bins

Number: ___ Colors: ____________________

- Clear boxes

Number: ___ Colors: ____________________

- Drawer dividers

Number: ___ Colors: ____________________

- Stackable drawers

Number: ___ Colors: ____________________

- Sliding basket drawers

Number: ___ Colors: ____________________

- Rack organizers

Number: ___ Colors: ____________________

- Pots and pans organizer

Number: ___ Colors: ____________________

- Cord organizer

Number: ___ Colors: ____________________

- Under sink organizer

Number: ___ Colors: ____________________

- Rotating turntable organizer

Number: ___ Colors: ____________________

- Shoe organizer

Number: ___ Colors: ____________________

- Under bed organizer

Number: ___ Colors: ____________________

- Hanging clothes organizers

Number: ___ Colors: ____________________

- Hangers

Number: ___ Colors: ____________________

- Storage cart

Number: ___ Colors: ____________________

- Underwear organizer

Number: ___ Colors: ____________________

- Spice rack organizer

Number: ___ Colors: ____________________

- Spice drawer organizer

Number: ___ Colors: ___________________

- Pre-labelled boxes/bins/baskets

Number: ___ Colors: ___________________

- Wall-mounted broom holder

Number: ___ Colors: ___________________

- Paper letter tray organizer

Number: ___ Colors: ___________________

- File holders/desk organizers

Number: ___ Colors: ___________________

- Bookends

Number: ___ Colors: ___________________

- Makeup organizer

Number: ___ Colors: ___________________

- Electronics organizer

Number: ___ Colors: ___________________

- Shower caddy

Number: ___ Colors: ____________________

Tips for Organizing Your Closet

As I mentioned at the beginning of the chapter, first, you have to look at the space available to you, then think about the different ways in which you can maximize the space. Here are some of my favorite tips for making your closet look beautiful and organized:

- Store out-of-season clothes out of sight in large boxes or bins. You can buy aesthetically pleasing clothes bins. Large hat boxes and gift boxes are also excellent options for storing out-of-season items away from sight.
- If possible, use the same type and color of hangers for your entire closet. For instance, if you use wooden hangers in white, stick with that. If you use beige velvet hangers, use the same for all your clothing items.
- Hang items like shirts, blouses, skirts, dresses, jackets, and trousers.
- T-shirts and workout clothes can be folded and stacked vertically inside organizer bins placed on the shelves of your closet.
- Group items of a similar type together. For instance, dresses can be one group, jackets can be another, etc.
- Create color blocks within each item category. To look visually pleasing, you should arrange clothes from light to dark.
- To maximize the shelving area, use stackable shelves. This way, you can easily take out whatever you need while making the best use of your space.

Exercise 10.2

Date:__________

Create a list of organizational supplies you need for organizing your closet area.

Develop a mental image of what you would like your fully organized closet to look like. If you are artistically inclined, drawing a blueprint will help you gain further clarity. Use the space below to make a rough drawing of what the closet will look like after you have finished organizing it.

Paste before and after pictures of your closet area below.

Tips for Organizing Your Kitchen and Pantry Area

A beautifully organized kitchen and pantry area can turn cooking into a delightful experience. Here are some tips to make this area beautiful, functional, and organized:

- Use clear containers made specifically for refrigerators to organize your refrigerator shelves. These clear containers come in all kinds of shapes and sizes. You want to arrange them to fill the majority of the space in your refrigerator; then, you can just keep stocking items inside them according to your needs. You can use these containers for versatile storage needs: one week, you can store a sandwich in a container, and another week, it can be utilized for storing potatoes.
- Divide the pantry into different sections. For instance, you can have a section for breakfast cereals, another for dry beans, another one for baking goods, etc. The idea is to group items of a similar nature together to make everything easily accessible. Labeling the containers can be extremely helpful in the pantry area. I personally love using chalkboard stickers on these containers, and I also use pre-labeled jars for various items. My pro tip for keeping your pantry area looking beautiful is to use the same type of storage containers in the entire area. For instance, if you use glass jars, try to use the same size and type of glass jars in the entire pantry.
- Place frequently used cooking utensils at easily accessible locations. Items you don't often use, like

baking utensils and tools, can be stored in less easily accessible areas.

- Use pots and pans dividers to keep them functionally organized.
- Use drawer dividers to neatly store all your cutlery and miscellaneous kitchen tools.
- Use plate holders to vertically stack your plates inside kitchen cabinets.
- Store items of a similar type together. For instance, bowls of the same size and color should be stacked together; the same idea applies to plates and other items.
- You can organize your spices either inside a drawer or on a spice rack. The spice rack can be stored inside a cabinet. I personally like to keep my countertops uncluttered and bare. This makes cleaning easy; plus, it gives me a sense of calm when I can walk inside my kitchen every morning to see it isn't looking "too busy."

Exercise 10.3

Date:_________

Create a list of organizational supplies you need for organizing your kitchen and pantry area.

Develop a mental image of what you would like the fully organized kitchen/pantry area to look like. If you are artistically inclined, drawing a blueprint will help you gain further clarity. Use the space below to make a rough drawing of what the kitchen will look like after you have finished organizing the area.

Paste before and after pictures of your kitchen and pantry area below.

Tips for Organizing Your Bathroom Area

We all love a beautiful bathroom that looks fit for Cleopatra! Yet, such a bathroom eludes most people. I've got some great ideas to make your bathrooms look and feel luxurious on any budget.

- Divide the items you use in the bathroom into different categories and assign a "home" for each category.
- Decide where the "home" for each item category should be, for instance, under the sink, in the shower area, inside the medicine cabinet, in the linen closet, etc.
- Use a shower caddy to store all your bath products.
- To make your bathroom more aesthetically pleasing, remove all packaging containers. Decant all items into clear plastic/glass or ceramic containers. If you are sharing the bathroom with others, then each person can have their own caddy with their own set of decanted products stored in clear containers; if you feel that would cause confusion, you can buy pre-packaged containers. This is the best tip for making any bathroom look instantly luxurious. Obviously, I do not recommend using glass containers in the bathroom if you have children around.
- Use the area under the sink to store frequently used items. But as I said in Book 1, be careful not to store anything there that can be impacted by moisture, like an electric shaver or any battery-operated device. Keep everything neatly categorized by storing

different types of items in color-coded bins/baskets/boxes.

- You can store items with their original packaging in closets and cabinets. This way, you can still access them easily, but the packaging isn't displayed inside the bathroom like an eyesore.
- Use the linen closet to store your sheets and towels. Again, use bins to store everything vertically.

Exercise 10.4

Date:__________

Create a list of organizational supplies you need for organizing your bathroom area.

Develop a mental image of what you would like the fully organized bathroom to look like. If you are artistically inclined, drawing a blueprint will help you gain further clarity. Use the space below to make a rough drawing of what your bathroom will look like after you have finished organizing it.

Paste before and after pictures of your bathroom area below.

Tips for Organizing Your Study/Home Office

A clean desk with minimum items on display induces a sense of calm and enables you to be at your creative best. Having a functionally organized and aesthetically pleasing home office becomes all the more essential if you are someone who, like me, works from home.

- Use metal bookends to keep books vertically stacked on shelves and other areas you like to display them. This way, you can pull out one book and shift the bookend a little so that the books still remain perfectly vertically stacked.
- Use filing cabinets or file storage boxes for storing all your files.
- Desk organizers can come in handy for keeping stationery and other such items beautifully displayed and easily accessible.
- Buy a document organizer and folders for storing all your important paperwork.
- Maximize drawer space by using drawer dividers. You can use adjustable drawer dividers that easily allow you to modify the layout whenever needed.

Exercise 10.5

Date:__________

Create a list of organizational supplies you need for organizing your study/home office area.

. . .

Develop a mental image of what you would like the fully organized study/office area to look like. If you are artistically inclined, drawing a blueprint will help you gain further clarity. Use the space below to make a rough drawing of what the area will look like after you have finished organizing it.

Paste before and after pictures of your study/home office area below.

Tips for Organizing Your Cleaning Supplies Aesthetically

While cleaning supplies play an essential role in helping us maintain a clean and tidy space, it can be difficult to keep them organized in a way that looks aesthetically pleasing. Let's explore some options for storing cleaning supplies in a more aesthetically pleasing manner.

- Store them behind closed doors whenever possible. This could mean making maximum use of the area under the sink or an extra storage cabinet.
- Prepare a cleaning caddy by placing all the cleaning supplies you need daily in the caddy. You can pull out this caddy and take it with you every day when you are ready to clean. You can buy a caddy with a handle for this purpose.
- Use wall-mounted broom organizers in storage closets to hang all your brooms and mops.
- Use cabinet door-mounted organizers for storing your kitchen and bathroom cleaning supplies.
- You can also consider decanting cleaning products into clear plastic containers or spray bottles if the labels and packaging boxes bother you too much.
- Keep all your cleaning supplies neatly organized in different categories. Use boxes/bins/baskets wherever necessary.

Exercise 10.6

Date:_________

Create a list of organizational supplies you need for organizing your cleaning supplies.

Develop a mental image of what you would like the fully organized cleaning supplies area to look like. If you are artistically inclined, drawing a blueprint will help you gain further clarity. Use the space below to make a rough drawing of what the area will look like after you have finished organizing it.

Paste before and after pictures of your cleaning supplies storage area below.

Chapter 11

Routines and Checklists

"With consistency and reps and routine you're going to achieve your goals and get where you want to be."

— Mandy Rose ("Routine Quotes," n.d.)

The best way to keep your house beautiful is by maintaining a regular routine of cleaning and tidying. You should have lists categorizing all the important tasks that need to be performed regularly. Maintaining lists of things that need to be done around the house is essential if you want to live in an aesthetically pleasing and highly functional home.

Don't Be a Perfectionist

I really want you to ditch your perfectionism when it comes to performing housework. You are never going to be able to do everything perfectly. As long as you are doing at least the basics regularly, you are doing well.

Also, you must keep your standards flexible for those times when your situation changes. For instance, having company over, the arrival of new babies, long working hours, stressful life events, etc. are all good reasons to allow your regular routine to be interrupted. During such times, you have to establish and define your priorities. Nothing matters more than the health, safety, and comfort of the people living in your home. In such times, clutter, organization, entertainment, and appearances can be allowed to take a backseat. You can always return back to your original schedule as soon as you start feeling ready for it. But don't be too hard on yourself. As I said earlier, the goal isn't to live in an uncluttered, beautiful home; your goal is to live a happy, peaceful, and beautiful life in a harmonious house that reflects your inner persona.

Stick to a minimal, workable routine when maintaining your ideal routine seems too hard to do. You are doing well if you and your family have healthy meals to eat, clean dishes to eat food from, and fresh clothes to wear. It is also a good idea to at least keep the bedroom vacuumed, dusted, and well-aired. Bedding should also be changed frequently to maintain hygiene.

Routines and Checklists

In this section, I will share with you some sample routines. Feel free to modify these to suit your individual needs, as some things may be relevant to you while others may not.

I strongly recommend that you photocopy or print these routines. Keep them handy to stay on top of your schedule and mark each item after you have completed it daily. You can use an online resource or an app on your phone to keep track of the tasks you have accomplished. You can also place your routines in a file with each routine stored securely in its own waterproof document sleeve. Use a dry erase marker to checkmark each item once the task has been completed. At the end of the day, you can wipe the waterproof sheet with a microfiber cloth. Use glass cleaning spray to remove any marker stains more neatly.

Daily Routine

- Make beds
- Place soiled clothes in laundry hamper and hang/fold all other clothes
- Run a fresh load of laundry. This can be either a daily task or a weekly one, depending upon the size of your household. Just stay on top of your laundry!
- Wipe phones with a microfiber cloth
- Clean computer surfaces and keyboards
- Change the water for flowers, remove wilted petals, and prune the ends
- Water the plants
- Clean all sinks at least once after use (including traps and drains)
- Clean the bathtub area after taking a shower/bath (including traps and drains)
- Clean bathroom counters and toilets
- Check/refill essential supplies in the bathroom (like soap, toilet paper, shampoo, conditioner, toothpaste, etc.)
- Put out fresh kitchen towels and place the used ones in the laundry hamper

- Prepare food and clean up afterward
- Wipe kitchen countertops after each use
- Wipe the stove area
- Run a load of dirty dishes in the dishwasher
- Put clean and dried dishes away
- Clean the floors in frequently used areas like the kitchen, living room, and main entryway
- Refill humidifiers and vaporizers (also, clean them if needed)
- Shopping for essentials and groceries (whenever necessary)
- Take out the trash and place fresh garbage bags in the trash containers
- Tidy for 20 minutes (place items back in their "home" + discard items that are no longer needed)

Weekly Routine

You can assign each major task to a specific day of the week. Dividing the list in this manner will help you accomplish multiple tasks without feeling overwhelmed. Once you have established a day for each major task of the week, it would be a good idea to stick to it long-term. Over time, you'll get accustomed to associating that specific day of the week with the task you have to perform.

What if you miss out on completing the task on the day assigned to it? In that case, simply perform the missed task along with the task listed for the next day.

Here is a list suggesting how you can use different days of the week to accomplish various tasks:

- Monday – Washing and ironing

- Tuesday – Miscellaneous odd jobs
- Wednesday – Minor housecleaning
- Thursday – Shopping for groceries and essentials
- Friday – Sorting through paper clutter; cleaning out handbags
- Saturday – Decluttering + organizing + major house cleaning
- Sunday – Holiday

Weekly Tasks Checklist

Here is a list of house cleaning chores you may want to perform weekly. Again, use your discretion to add or remove items from the list. You can assign the tasks to different days of the week to suit your personal schedule and needs.

- Change bed linens once or twice every week
- Wash all washable floors
- Vacuum rugs, carpeted surfaces, lampshades, and upholstered furniture
- Vacuum faux flowers and other home decor items
- Replace wilted flowers with fresh ones
- Dust all surfaces that require dusting, including light fixtures, picture frames, and artwork
- Wipe doors and doorknobs
- Wipe all closet and cabinet doors
- Dust windows and wipe the surface of windows
- Wipe all mirrors
- Deep clean the bathroom (including all areas like sink, bathtub, toilet, wall tiles, toothbrush holders, cabinet exteriors and shelves, floor, mirror, etc.)
- Deep clean the kitchen (remove unwanted/wipe items from the refrigerator, wipe refrigerator

surfaces, wipe the exterior of ovens/microwaves, clean sinks, tabletops, countertops, scrub floors)
- Clean humidifiers and air conditioner filters (if needed)
- Wash all combs and hairbrushes
- Take clothes to the dry cleaners

Monthly/Quarterly/Seasonal Checklist

Here is a checklist for recommended tasks that should be performed monthly or quarterly. Some of the tasks need to be performed each season.

- Launder mattress covers and pillow covers (the innermost pillowcase, inside which the actual pillow rests, not the case that matches your bedsheets) (monthly)
- Deep clean the entryway (monthly)
- Clean under heavy furniture and appliances (quarterly)
- Declutter and organize the garden area (quarterly or whenever needed)
- Dust blinds and all hard-to-reach areas that collect dust (monthly)
- Deep clean the oven and microwave (depending upon usage, you can either have this as a monthly task or a quarterly task)
- Rotate all mattresses (quarterly)
- Clean all fans (quarterly)
- Wax floors (quarterly or whenever needed)
- Wax wooden surfaces (quarterly or whenever needed)

- Declutter and reorganize all frequently used cabinets, drawers, and closets (monthly or quarterly)
- Give away unused/unworn items (monthly)
- Clean the garage (quarterly)

Annual/Semiannual Checklist

This is a list of tasks that should be performed annually or semiannually; use your discretion to decide what works best for you. Of course, some of these items may not apply to you, so feel free to edit the list to suit your needs and living situation.

- Get blankets, comforters, and quilts dry-cleaned. You can also wash them if the manufacturer's instructions prescribe that.
- Clean and store out-of-season clothes away from sight; replace with seasonal clothing (every spring and fall season)
- Polish and clean all silverware
- Clean and polish all precious jewelry items
- Deep clean all walls, floors, and ceilings
- Clean the basement area
- Vacuum books
- Shampoo upholstery and rugs
- Empty and deep clean all drawers, closets, and cabinets
- Wash blinds and windows
- Wash or dry-clean curtains and draperies
- Organize and declutter gadgets
- Donate or discard gadgets and tools that are no longer needed

Checklist for Those Days When You Can't Do the Full Routine

Use this checklist whenever you are lacking the time, energy, or willpower needed to perform your regular routine.

- Make the bed (change bed linen at least once a week)
- Wash dirty dishes
- Prepare food you can cook quickly or use pre-packaged meals
- Restock essential pantry items
- Wipe kitchen countertops
- Scrub the kitchen sink
- Clean the toilet
- Wipe bathroom countertop
- Dust and vacuum only those areas where you and other family members spend the maximum amount of their time
- Run a fresh load of laundry
- Put things back in place after each use

For Those Times When You are Feeling Overwhelmed...

We all go through those times when things feel way too overwhelming. During such times, it's worth considering outsourcing some of the housekeeping work. If you can fit it into your budget, hiring cleaning help is a good idea. You can call a cleaning service company in your local area and have a maid come in for a day (or half a day) to help you out with the weekly cleaning tasks.

The checklists will come in really handy when you assign tasks to someone else. Hired cleaners will know exactly what is expected of them, which will help you maintain the cleanliness and tidiness of your space.

You can also consider hiring someone to help do the annual/semi-annual deep cleaning tasks. To save time on grocery shopping, you can start ordering groceries online. If you are very particular about using the freshest produce, then you can also foster an agreement with a local farm to deliver fresh produce once every week. Try to produce less laundry, and if you already have a large pile of it, then consider sending it out to a laundry service company.

When the situation is very serious (like during a major illness, childbirth, or death in the family), speak up and ask for the help of close friends and family. Most of the time, our loved ones are eager to help us; they just don't know how to do it. Tell them honestly how you would like them to help you, and this can significantly ease your burden.

Exercise 11.1

Date:__________

Photocopy/print the above checklists or refer to the free printable checklists; the link is at the front of this book. You can also create your own using the checklists in this chapter as an inspiration. Also, don't forget to download the 7 Tips to Declutter Your Life free eBook for some additional decluttering hacks; the link is at the front of this book!

You can digitally track the completion of each task, or you can use a file to store your checklists. Place each checklist inside a waterproof, transparent document sleeve and mark each task with a dry erase pen after it has been completed. Erase the markings when you need to use the checklist again. Alternatively, you can use whiteboards to write down your checklists and mark your progress.

Chapter 12

Pro Tips on Living a Clutter-Free Life

"In the never-ending battle between order and chaos, clutter sides with chaos every time. Anything that you possess that does not add to your life or your happiness eventually becomes a burden."

— John Robbins (Hage, 2021)

The best strategy for tackling clutter is to simply prevent it from entering your life and your physical space. Easier said than done; I know! Learning to distinguish clutter from the items we truly love and value is an art in itself. But the good news is that you get better at it the more frequently you practice.

Questions to Ask Yourself Before Buying/Bringing in Any New Item

It does take a tremendous amount of self-reflection and self-awareness to prevent clutter from entering your home. To ease the process of identifying potential clutter before it enters your space, here is a checklist of questions you may want to ask yourself before buying or bringing in any new item.

- Do I really need this?
- Am I buying this because it serves a definite purpose for me, or am I feeling tempted to buy it because it's being offered at a discounted price?
- How many times do I intend to use it?
- Where will I store it? (You should be able to clearly visualize a "home" for each item that you add to your space.)
- What will happen to it when it is no longer useful to me?
- Is it truly worth the money I'm willing to spend on it?
- What's going to be its cost per wear/cost per use?
- Is there another item that better serves my needs and preferences?
- Am I buying this just because it's cheaper than the item I actually want?
- Would I really regret not buying it?
- Can I postpone buying it and take my time to decide whether or not this is something truly valuable to me?
- For how long do I see myself using this item?
- Are there any maintenance costs associated with keeping this item in a functional/useful condition?
- What is the total cost of this product if I add the maintenance cost to the initial cost of the product?
- Do I see myself taking good care of this item?
- Does it match my personality/taste/style?

Exercise 12.1

Date:________

Create a copy of this checklist and keep it with you at all times, whether in paper form or in digital form. Before making any purchase, ask yourself these questions. You'll realize that a lot of items you feel tempted to buy are things you don't actually need.

Marketers understand the lure of discount prices. While we think we are saving money, most of the time, we are really just spending money on things that neither make us truly happy nor meet any specific need of ours.

Using this checklist will help you save time, money, and energy. You'll buy less, but you'll buy more of the things that truly add value to your life. You'll feel good about your ability as a decision-maker. Since you are judiciously assessing each potential purchase, you are less likely to make blunders in the form of accumulated clutter.

Buy High-Quality Items that Last Longer

The allure of discount prices is unmistakable. We go to the store to buy one shirt but end up returning home with four t-shirts because we managed to get all four at the price of one! Sounds like a great deal. Isn't it? Not really! You have to start thinking about the *true* cost of an item based on how much it costs you per use/wear. If you are buying a $10 t-shirt that looks decent for only two wears, that's a splurge. On the other hand, an organic cotton shirt sold at $60 that will last you a couple of years is a steal because the cost per wear is much lower.

Another important thing to consider is how the item makes you feel when you are wearing/using it. A low-quality discount-store t-shirt is unlikely to make you feel like a million bucks, but a high-quality shirt made out of premium materials that lasts a long time gives you the feeling of being on top of the world.

Start investing in items that make you feel good and add real value to your life. Don’t let discounts and price reductions tempt you, or you’ll just keep accumulating more clutter. It’s totally worth saving up and splurging more on items you truly value and like having. A purchase isn’t really extravagant or unjustified if it significantly improves the quality of your life or how you feel about yourself.

Your goal should be to live in a house and work in a space surrounded only by those items you truly love. You deserve to live in such a home! It’s very difficult to have a clutter problem when you follow the basic principle of buying only those things that truly add value to your life.

Exercise 12.2

Date:__________

Create a wishlist of items you truly want to buy. For a few moments, forget about the sticker price of each item. Just think about what you would buy if money wasn’t a constraint. Identify a few items that are currently within your budget and create a strategy for buying them. (For instance, you may have to forgo buying several cheap items in order to spend money on one item you truly want.)

Before making the final purchase, use the checklist from the previous section to identify whether or not this item would be truly valuable to you.

Conclusion

Thank you for placing your trust in me! I really hope this book has been a life-changing experience for you. If you have steadily worked through the teachings of each chapter and diligently completed every single exercise listed in this book, I am sure you have strong results to show by now.

If you haven't yet gotten the results you are looking for, it's okay! Just go back to the first chapter and slowly work through the contents of this book, implementing just one thing at a time. Every person is different. Hence, the time required by each person to get the results they are looking for is also going to be different. As I said at the beginning of the book, the most important thing is to be loving and compassionate to yourself.

Also, don't forget that decluttering and organizing are processes that never end. No matter how many times you declutter a specific area, it may become cluttered again. This is especially true if you have a large family in which each family member has a different temperament.

Remember that no matter how bad the clutter looks, you will never go back to square one. When you had a serious clutter problem, you didn't have all the tools, tips, techniques, tricks, and methods that you now have. By applying what you have learned through this book in a systematic manner, you can quickly declutter and reorganize any space.

Decluttering and organizing must happen regularly. This is why I've added them to the routines checklists (which I hope you are using regularly). The journey is the goal; you've got to start loving and enjoying it. Look at decluttering and organizing as acts of love and gratitude towards the items that serve you.

Thank You

Thank you for purchasing my book.

You chose this book. Thank you for picking it! And thanks for reading it all the way through. I hope you received value from the book and found the decluttering advice to be helpful.

Could you please consider writing a review of my book on the platform?

Writing a review is the best and easiest way to support people like me who self-publish books. Your review helps other people find my work and enjoy it, too!

It will help me write the kind of books that will help you get the results you want. It would mean a lot to me to hear from you.

>> Leave a review on Amazon US <<
>> Leave a review on Amazon UK <<

References

110 Bob Proctor quotes from the inspirational self-help author. Free Ideas For Family Fun & Learning. (n.d.). Retrieved March 30, 2022, from https://kidadl.com/articles/bob-proctor-quotes-from-the-inspirational-self-help-author

28 amazing quotes that will inspire you to get organized. Order Your Life. (2018, February 1). Retrieved March 31, 2022, from https://orderyourlife.com/blogs/blog/28-amazing-quotes-that-will-inspire-you-to-get-organized

A thing worth doing. Society of Gilbert Keith Chesterton. (2012, April 29). Retrieved March 30, 2022, from https://www.chesterton.org/a-thing-worth-doing/

Abramson, A. (2019, September 3). *10 quotes that will empower you to declutter anything.* Apartment Therapy. Retrieved March 30, 2022, from https://www.apartmenttherapy.com/inspirational-quotes-decluttering-36638725

Cirillo, F. (2018). *The pomodoro technique.* Random House UK.

Cleaning. Wikipedia. (2022, February 28). Retrieved March 31, 2022, from https://en.wikipedia.org/wiki/Cleaning

Clear, J. (2020, February 4). *How long does it actually take to form a new habit?* JamesClear.com. Retrieved March 31, 2022, from https://jamesclear.com/new-habit

Fields Millburn, J., & Nicodemus, R. (2019, August 7). *Getting rid of just-in-case items: 20 dollars, 20 minutes.* The Minimalists. Retrieved March 31, 2022, from https://www.theminimalists.com/jic/

Habit quotes. Brainy Quote. (n.d.). Retrieved March 31, 2022 from https://www.brainyquote.com/topics/habit-quotes

Hage, J. (2021, November 24). *Motivational quotes for cleaning: 20 positive clean home sayings.* Filling the Jars. Retrieved March 31, 2022, from https://www.fillingthejars.com/motivational-quotes-for-cleaning/

Lao Tzu quote. Brainy Quote. (n.d.). Retrieved March 30, 2022 from https://www.brainyquote.com/quotes/lao_tzu_137141

Mackey, M. (2022, January 13). *100 quotes about self-care, because being good to yourself has never been more important.* Parade. Retrieved March 31, 2022, from https://parade.com/1070248/maureenmackey/self-care-quotes/

Our favorite clutter quotes: Unmade decisions and procrastination. Postconsumers. (2020, August 24). Retrieved March 30, 2022, from https://www.postconsumers.com/2015/01/09/clutter-quotes-6/

Pathak, A. (2021, August 27). *150 epic goal setting quotes that will change your life.* Vantage Circle HR Blog. Retrieved

March 30, 2022, from https://blog.vantagecircle.com/goal-setting-quotes/

Routine quotes. BrainyQuote. (n.d.). Retrieved March 31, 2022, from https://www.brainyquote.com/topics/routine-quotes

Smart criteria. Wikipedia. (2022, February 24). Retrieved March 30, 2022, from https://en.wikipedia.org/wiki/SMART_criteria

Tidy. Cambridge English Dictionary. (n.d.). Retrieved March 31, 2022, from https://dictionary.cambridge.org/dictionary/english/tidy

Tony Robbins quote. AZ Quotes. (n.d.). Retrieved March 30, 2022, from https://www.azquotes.com/quote/1457094

Vision quotes. Brainy Quote. (n.d.). Retrieved March 31, 2022 from https://www.brainyquote.com/topics/vision-quotes

Vision quotes. Goodreads. (n.d.). Retrieved March 31, 2022 from https://www.goodreads.com/quotes/tag/vision

Printed in Great Britain
by Amazon

35331758R00099